THE
Power
OF A
Positive
M♥M

THE Power OF A Positive MOM

Karol Ladd

HOWARD
PUBLISHING CO.

Our purpose at Howard Publishing is to:
- *Increase faith* in the hearts of growing Christians
- *Inspire holiness* in the lives of believers
- *Instill hope* in the hearts of struggling people everywhere

Because He's coming again!

The Power of a Positive Mom © 2001 by Karol Ladd
All rights reserved. Printed in the United States of America

Published by Howard Publishing Co., Inc.,
3117 North 7th Street, West Monroe, Louisiana 71291-2227

02 03 04 05 06 07 08 09 10   10 9 8 7 6 5

Edited by Michele Buckingham
Interior design by Stephanie Denney

Library of Congress Cataloging-in-Publication Data
Ladd, Karol.
    The power of a positive mom / Karol Ladd.
        p. cm.
    Includes bibliographical references.
    ISBN 1-58229-163-2
        1. Mothers—Religious life. 2. Motherhood—Religious aspects—Christianity.
    3. Parenting—Religious aspects—Christianity. I. Title.

BV4529.18 .L33 2001
248.8'431—dc21
                                                        2001016818

Scripture quotations not otherwise marked are from the Holy Bible, New International Version. Copyright © 1973, 1978, 1984 International Bible Society. Used by permission of Zondervan Bible Publishers. All rights reserved.

Scripture quotations marked NKJV are taken from the New King James Version. Copyright © 1979, 1980, 1982 by Thomas Nelson, Inc. Used by permission. All rights reserved.

Scripture quotations marked PHILLIPS are from J. B. Phillips: The New Testament in Modern English, Revised Edition, copyright © J. B. Phillips 1958, 1960, 1972. Used by permission of Macmillan Publishing Co., Inc.

Dedication

To my precious family, Curt, Grace, and Joy.
Thank you for your faithful love, encouragement, and support.
You are truly God's gift to me.

To my dad, Garry Kinder, whose positive attitude,
example, and leadership influenced me to reach greater heights.

To my faithful prayer warriors, Nancy, Lisa, and Carol.
Your fervent prayers avail much! I truly appreciate your
dedication to this ministry.

And to my supportive friends, Beth, Leslie, Amy, and Tracy.
Thank you for your positive encouragement.

Thank you, Howard Publishing and Philis Boultinghouse,
for your excellence in publishing Christian books.

Most importantly, to our heavenly Father, who gives us the
strength and power to be positive moms each day.

About the Author

Karol Ladd has been making a positive impact in the lives of kids for many years. Formerly a teacher, Karol is now a writer and speaker. Most importantly, she is a wife and mother. Karol has written more than ten books that share creative and fresh ideas for families. Her books include *Parties with a Purpose, Party Mix, Summer with a Smile, Scream Savers, Table Talk, Fun House,* and The Glad Scientist series. Her energetic personality and informative ideas make her a popular speaker with numerous women's groups and mothers' organizations. Karol is the cofounder of a character-building club for young girls called USA Sonshine Girls. Karol's rich background also includes working in children's ministry and with Christian camps and serving on the board of several pro-family organizations.

Contents

Contents

Principle #4: The Power of Strong Relationships

Principle #5: The Power of Your Example

Principle #6: The Power of Strong Moral Standards

Principle #7: The Power of Love and Forgiveness

Introduction

You Can Do It!
Making a Positive Difference

The wise woman builds her house.
—Proverbs 14:1

Every child needs a positive push in life. An enthusiastic word, a loving smile, or a prayer of support may be just the encouragement a young person needs to send him or her off in the right direction.

That's where mothers come in. As moms, we have the opportunity every day to boost our children onward and upward. Ours is a highly influential job. Through our affirmative support and loving care, we are in a unique position to help our children reach for their dreams and achieve their God-given potential.

Unfortunately, in the day-to-day struggles of motherhood, our good intentions toward our kids can seem to fly out the window. We may start off the day with a fresh outlook and high expectations, but midway through the second temper tantrum of the morning (theirs, not ours), we somehow lose our handle on the uplifting encouragement we intended to share. How can we be positive when we often feel like the greatest portion of our day is spent correcting, scolding, and trying to avert minor disasters? It doesn't help that we're distracted from

1

our efforts to be affirming by the daily chores of running errands, doing laundry, and putting dinner on the table.

I truly believe that most of us start out as positive mothers when that little newborn baby is first laid in our arms. It is easy to look down at that bundle of precious potential and fill our minds with hopes and dreams of what he or she will one day become (through our guidance and influence, of course). But in the aftermath of those blissful moments we begin to deal with the business of everyday life and child rearing, and we discover that it is more challenging to be a positive parent than we ever dreamed.

This book is written to help every mother rediscover and recapture that spirit of affirmation and encouragement—that sense of great expectation and purpose and possibility we all felt in the beginning—even in the midst of the everyday struggles of raising kids. You can do it! These are four powerful words. Our children need to hear them quite often. But today I want to say them to *you*.

Yes, you can do it! With God's help and with his Holy Spirit living inside you, you can be, as the writer of Proverbs says, "the wise woman [who] builds her house" (Proverbs 14:1). The seven principles I offer in this book are meant to help you recognize the amazing power that God has put in the hands of positive mothers—and to inspire you to become the positive mom you want and need to be. Each chapter is filled with quotes, scriptures, and real-life examples designed to encourage you and spur you on.

At the close of each chapter is a section called "Power Point" with a suggestion for further Bible study, a model prayer, and an activity to reinforce the principles you've just learned. After all, God's power is not in the reading; it's in the *doing!* These Power Point sections lend themselves well to group study with fellow mothers. In fact, studying this book and completing the Power Point steps with other mothers is a great way to find mutual encouragement and support as you seek to become a more positive mom.

Pass It On

I don't know about you, but I was blessed to have been raised by a positive mom and dad. My mother passed away several years ago, but her discipline and godly character were powerful examples in my life. She was a kind woman with a servant's heart who prayed continually for her family and friends. For his part, my dad always taught his kids to look at the positive and not dwell on the negative. Even today he is an encourager—always wearing a smile on his face and ready to speak a good word. I learned a great deal from my parents' positive influence, and part of my desire in writing this book is to pass on to you some of the wisdom they taught me.

Maybe you had positive parents too. Maybe not. Either way, you and I both have the ultimate positive parent: God, our heavenly Father. The principles in this book are powerful and true, not because I had great parents or because I'm an extraordinary mother myself (although I try my best). Rather, they are supremely powerful and absolutely true because they come from God's Word.

I've spoken about these principles in women's meetings for several years, and I've always enjoyed hearing feedback from women who say, " 'The Power of a Positive Mom' has made me a better mother." Interestingly enough, I found myself saying these same words as I searched the Scriptures further and did more research to write this book.

I grew to have a deeper prayer life while writing chapter 6 and studying the faith-filled prayers of George Muller. I became more positive and thankful as I considered the importance of "an attitude of gratitude" while writing chapter 10. I added several time-honored traditions to our family celebrations after working on chapter 16. Throughout the writing of the entire book I learned to encourage my children in more effective ways through my words, actions, and example.

I'm just a fellow journeyman (or should I say journey*mom*) in this adventure of motherhood. The principles in this book have made a strong impact on my parenting abilities, and I believe they will do the same for you. I've written in a "mother-friendly" style, short and to the point, because I realize most moms have only small snippets of spare time to take in a chapter or two. So while the kids are napping or playing happily at your feet, take a moment to relish and reflect on the words of refreshment in the pages that follow. You will find the boost of encouragement you need to make it through the rest of the day.

We live in a rapidly changing world. The values that our mothers and fathers grew up with are no longer being taught in the public arena. We find negative influences and declining moral values every where we look, from television to movies to magazines. Our kids desperately need the positive influence of mothers who love them, who love God, and who know how to tap into the power that only he gives.

The seven principles in this book will help you become not only a positive influence in your home, but also in your community—and possibly in the society at large. As you draw upon the ideas presented in these pages, remember that you can make a positive difference in your world one child at a time. There has never been a more critical time for children to experience the power of a positive mom!

Portrait
OF A
Positive
MOM

Adam named his wife Eve,
because she would become the mother of all the living.
—Genesis 3:20

*When Eve was brought unto Adam, he became filled
with the Holy Spirit, and gave her the most sanctified,
the most glorious of appelations. He called her Eva, that is to say,
the Mother of All. He did not style her wife, but simply mother,—
mother of all living creatures. In this consists the glory
and the most precious ornament of woman.*
—Martin Luther

Influence beyond Measure
Never Underestimate the Power of a Mother

She is clothed with strength and dignity; she can laugh at the days to come. She speaks with wisdom, and faithful instruction is on her tongue.... Her children arise and call her blessed.
—Proverbs 31:25–26, 28

Mothers possess a rare form of wisdom. We know important information that others don't—such as the exact location of the rest room in every grocery store in town and the correct color of cough medicine to administer to a child with a dry, hacking cough. The rest of humanity may not know how to cut sandwiches into animal shapes or which fast-food restaurants have the best playgrounds, but mothers know. And moms are keenly aware that a chocolate ice cream cone cannot be consumed by a preschooler without leaving its mark on a freshly cleaned outfit or finely upholstered furniture. Others seem oblivious to that fact (especially dads!).

Obviously, we mothers make up a highly informed segment of society. Some days we may wish we did not possess such experiential knowledge, but the truth is we wouldn't trade this job for the world. It's the toughest job we ever loved!

Motherhood transforms naive, inexperienced young ladies into wise, accomplished women who command respect. Maternal love strengthens us and helps us grow into selfless, thoughtful, and giving adults. I like how author Susan Lapinski describes it: "I guess what I've discovered is the humanizing effect of children in my life, stretching me, humbling me. Maybe my thighs aren't as thin as they used to be; maybe my getaways aren't as glamorous. Still, I like the woman that motherhood has helped me to become."[1]

Yes, being a mom brings out the best in us!

Granted, the work schedule for a mother is a bit challenging: twenty-four hours a day, seven days a week, fifty-two weeks a year, with no weekends or holidays off. Some people would balk at such impossible hours, but not mothers! God has given us an inexplicable strength—a strength beyond our own strength—that allows us to tend to the multiple needs and cares of our precious charges. Like the Energizer bunny, we just keep going and going despite midnight feedings, sleepless slumber parties, twice-a-week soccer practices (plus a game on Saturday), and overdue science projects. It generally requires a doctor's orders for a mom to take "sick leave."

Cathy is a good example. A mother of two preschoolers, she had rarely taken a leave of absence from her job as a mother. But when she found herself restricted to bed rest under a doctor's care, she called her in-laws to come to the rescue. Before her replacements arrived, however, her three-year-old son, Ryan, approached her and said with deep concern, "Mommy what are we going to do? Who is going to feed us and put us to bed and play with us?" Tears filled his little eyes. "I need you!" he cried.

Ryan recognized the truth that when mom is off-duty, things just aren't the same. He was consoled only when he was told that Grandma was on her way. At least his grandmother was an experienced mother!

The Worth of a Mom

A study recently conducted by Edelman Financial Services tried to identify the many occupations that a typical mother might be said to hold over the course of a year. The researchers also examined salary data supplied by the U.S. Bureau of Labor Statistics, trade groups, and human resource and staffing firms. Putting all the information together, Edelman estimated that a mother's worth is approximately $507,000 per year! Here is a breakdown of the various tasks typically performed by a mother and the corresponding median salaries:

Animal Caretaker $17,500

Executive Chef $40,000

Computer Systems Analyst $44,000

Financial Manager $39,000

Food/Beverage Service Worker $20,000

General Office Clerk $19,000

Registered Nurse $35,000

Management Analyst $41,000

Childcare Worker $13,000

Housekeeper $9,000

Psychologist $29,000

Bus Driver $32,400

Elementary School Principal $58,600

Dietitian/Nutritionist $41,600

Property Manager $22,600

Social Worker $30,000

Recreation Worker $15,500

The Edelman study suggested that since a mother wears many hats and is on duty twenty-four hours a day, she deserves a full-time, annual salary for all seventeen positions. And since the retirement, health, and insurance benefits that workers in these positions typically receive were not factored in, the figures should actually be much higher![2]

Quite a flattering list, don't you think? But I noticed that a few items were left out of the calculations. For example:

Kissing a boo-boo . . . . .Priceless

Fixing a favorite meal just the way they like it . . . . .Priceless

Making them feel special on their birthdays . . . . .Priceless

Getting up during the night for feedings or illnesses . . . .Priceless

Adjudicating sibling disputes .Priceless

Searching the entire house for a lost gerbil . . . . .Priceless

Cheering enthusiastically from the sidelines . . . . .Priceless

Scratching their backs while they lie in bed . . . . .Priceless

Baking warm cookies for an after-school snack . . . . . . .Priceless

Telling stories at bedtime . . . . .Priceless

Holding their hands during vaccinations . . . . .Priceless

Giving a hug, a smile, a word of encouragement . . . . . .Priceless

There are some things money just can't buy! While Edelman's research may have been on the right track, the truth is a mother's worth is incalculable. Few can duplicate our loving touch. What price tag can be placed on the sense of warmth and comfort we bring to our homes? On the feeling of protection and safety our children enjoy just because we're nearby? On our uncanny ability to sense our children's needs before they even ask?

Recently I asked a small group of mothers, "What makes a mother priceless?" One woman responded, "Nobody but a mom can tell when her child is about to throw up!" Who can calculate the worth of that kind of "mother's intuition"?

Tuning Out Popular Opinion

But the world does not necessarily recognize the unique value of motherhood. In fact, we have to fight hard not to be discouraged by current cultural trends that tend to devalue a mother's role and down-play her influence in the lives of her children. Modern society tells us three myths:

Myth #1: Genetics and Peer Pressure—Not Mothers—Influence Children Most

In her recent book *The Nurture Assumption: Why Children Turn Out the Way They Do* (Free Press, 1998), author Judith Rich Harris argues that nothing parents do or say will make much difference in influencing their children's personality, behavior, values, or intelligence. She concludes that genetics and peer pressure are the main factors contributing to the way children turn out. Parents are overrated, in her opinion.

Many experts on children and family issues do not agree with Harris's premise, however. "*The Nurture Assumption* is so disturbing," responds Dr. T. Berry Brazelton, renowned professor of pediatrics at Harvard Medical School. "It devalues what parents are trying to do. To say that they don't matter, it's frightening. Then parents may say, 'If I don't matter, why should I bother?' "[3]

Let me state here unequivocally: Parents do matter! A shifting culture and an increasingly humanistic world-view do not change the fact that a mother has always had—and will continue to have—a powerful impact on the development of her children. Certainly peer groups and genetics play a part in what kind of adults children turn out to be; but it is the parents' involvement that guides their children's interests and influences the direction of their young lives.

We need look no further than the Bible to see that God has given parents the job of training and teaching their children. In Deuteronomy 6:4–7, Moses charges the Israelites to faithfully impress God's commandments on their children's hearts: "Hear, O Israel: The

LORD our God, the LORD is one. Love the LORD your God with all your heart and with all your soul and with all your strength. These commandments I give you today are to be upon your hearts. Impress them on your children. Talk about them when you sit at home and when you walk along the road, when you lie down and when you get up."

Clearly God places in the hands of parents—not peers, not school-teachers, not government officials, or anyone else—the responsibility for teaching their children to love God and obey his Word. And as parents we have been specially empowered by God to pass on his commandments from generation to generation.

Myth #2: Motherhood Causes Women to Miss Out on the Exciting Things in Life

Modern society is rampant with self-centered philosophies of "self-improvement" and "self-actualization." We are bombarded daily with messages that tell us we should look out for number one and pursue our own interests and goals at any cost. This pervasive thinking, by implying that the selflessness of motherhood is not a worthy investment of our time and effort, often creates feelings of inadequacy in moms.

The underlying myth is that if we endeavor to be attentive mothers, we are missing out in life. Not so! Life *begins* with motherhood. What could be more invigorating, more life-giving, than a house full of energetic teenagers wanting to be fed or a handful of toddlers wanting to play hide and seek or a newborn baby wanting to be held?

Besides, as Jesus said in Matthew 10:39, "Whoever finds his life will lose it, and whoever loses his life for my sake will find it." Committing ourselves to love and care for our children as God commands—even if it means putting their needs above our own time and time again—is the way to a full and abundant life. Motherhood has this kind of selfless love built into the job description. I can assure you, we aren't the ones missing out!

Myth #3: Being a Mother Is a Waste of a Woman's Talents and Abilities

Certain women's movements today deny the significance of motherhood, asserting that our talents and abilities could be put to better use. But the truth is motherhood is not only a good use of our talents and abilities, it actually *increases* and *expands* them.

Being a mother broadens our world-view and opens our hearts to a deeper compassion and love for others. It constantly exposes us to new challenges and stretches us to learn new skills. Where else but in motherhood can a woman learn to effectively juggle five tasks at once? A typical mother can cook dinner, answer the telephone, and help with the homework while feeding the baby and scolding the dog. She can work at the hospital, shop for the household, do a couple of loads of laundry, write the bills, and still show affection for each of her loved ones. Amazing!

And remember Edelman's list of occupational roles filled by a mother over a year's time? Where else could a woman get such extensive on-the-job training?

Still, we often feel put to the challenge when someone asks, "And, what do *you* do?" Unfortunately, because of the way society thinks, it seems shallow to answer, "I'm a mother." Even though we know that motherhood is a high and important calling, we feel as though we must be able to list several substantial interests outside the home to satisfy our inquirers. It used to be that our occupation was spoken of with respect and honor; now it's treated as a mere accessory in the ensemble of life!

For the hand that rocks the cradle is the hand that rules the world. —W. S. Ross

I love the story of the mother who was approached by a young lady conducting a survey in a shopping mall. The interviewer asked the typical question, "What is your occupation?" Feeling a bit bold on this particular day, this astute mom responded, "I'm a manager for human resources and development." The young lady hesitated for a moment, then slowly wrote down the important-sounding title on her clipboard.

"And what exactly does your job entail?" she asked.

The mother's response was priceless: "My job requires continuous research and management both in the office and out in the field *[translation: in the house and out in the backyard]*. Currently, I am busy with three important case studies *[translation: I have two sons and a daughter]*. It is a demanding job, and I often work around the clock to cover all of my responsibilities. Although the monetary compensation is virtually nonexistent, the rewards and satisfaction go far beyond words."

The researcher looked at her with great respect and continued with the rest of the questions. When the survey was finished, the mother smiled down at her three young case studies. Then she led them out of the mall and happily treated them to a power lunch at a local fast-food facility.

Now that's what I call job confidence!

We, too, can be confident in the work we do as moms, knowing that we are making a difference every day in the lives of the children God has placed in our care. Whether we spend a major portion of our day at an office, a school, a hospital, a store, a factory, or at home, we are first and foremost mothers—and we are continuously building values and vision into the lives of our kids.

Sure, it's easy to become overwhelmed and unduly influenced by the expectations of our culture. But don't buy the lies! Hold on to what

No language can express the power and beauty and heroism of a mother's love. —Edwin H. Chapin

you know deep within your heart: You are absolutely *essential* in your home and in the lives of your kids. Your job has more than monetary value; it has eternal worth!

Remembering Our Employer

Take a moment now to reflect on the day you first added the word *mother* to your job title. It was on that day that you began a new and unique journey into the unknown. You took on a monumental obligation and trust, agreeing to a lifelong commitment to love and care for that new person God brought into your life. You probably felt inadequate at the time, but day by day you grew in wisdom, strength, and ability to match the challenges of your new role.

The truth is, *mother* describes not only what we do, but who we are. From the moment children were first introduced into our lives, we became new people—women with greater purpose, responsibility, and significance.

But if motherhood is our job, for whom do we work? Do we work to please the people of this world—a society that tells us we're unimportant, even unnecessary? Do we serve only our husband and children? Or are we working to honor our own needs?

Colossians 3:17 gives us the answer. "And whatever you do," the apostle Paul writes, "whether in word or in deed, do it all in the name of the Lord Jesus, giving thanks to God the Father through him." Paul continues in verses 23 and 24: "Whatever you do, work at it with all your heart, as working for the Lord, not for men, since you know that you will receive an inheritance from the Lord as a reward. It is the Lord Christ you are serving."

Our work is for the Lord. It is ultimately God we are pleasing as we devote ourselves to our families. It is God who will reward us one day for our untiring effort. If we were working for people in this world, we would no doubt want recognition or pay for our services. But ours is a higher calling. We are not working for money or accolades on earth; we are working with all our heart for the Lord. In fact, our entire job is done from the heart, rooted in the motherly love God has given us for our children.

Dear friend, you and I can go forward with complete job confidence. After all, we work for the greatest employer in the universe! Our work as mothers does matter—because it matters to God. We can wear the title with humility and honor, recognizing that we have the power to influence and mold our children like the precious pieces of human clay that they are.

Listen to the words of this insightful poem:

I took a piece of plastic clay
And idly fashioned it one day;
And as my fingers pressed it still,
It moved and yielded at my will.

I came again when days were past,
The form I gave it still did last
And as my fingers pressed it still,
I could change that form no more at will.

I took a piece of living clay,
And gently formed it day by day,
And molded with my power and art,
A young child's soft and yielding heart.

I came again when days were gone;
It was a man I looked upon,
He still that early impress bore,
And I could change it never more.[4]

It's true: Every new mother holds in her arms a precious bundle of malleable potential waiting to be molded into flourishing adulthood through her tender, loving care. Our job must never be taken lightly! We have a great responsibility—both to God and to our children. As we understand the impact that our words and actions have on the lives of our kids, we realize the monumental nature of our task. But God never gives us a job he doesn't first equip us to do. As mothers, we have been specially created to influence the lives of the generations that follow.

Consider my friend, Victor Caballero Jr. Victor juggles two demanding jobs. He is a probation officer for a juvenile court during the day and a gymnastics coach in the evenings and on weekends. Victor was one of ten children, raised from his youth by both his mother and grandmother in a household characterized by both strict discipline and unconditional love. He credits these two women with the strength and determination he learned as a young man and which continue to serve him well now.

More than anything else, Victor says, his mother and grandmother taught him the "wisdom of compassion" and how to truly care for others. With great insight, Victor adds, "If anyone understands pain and strength, it is a mother. My mother and grandmother endured much pain in their lives, yet they were incredible pillars of strength mixed with kindness."

Victor is not alone in recognizing the valuable contribution of the women in his life. Men and women throughout history have given their mothers acclaim and credit for the meaningful encouragement and direction they provided.

Abraham Lincoln, for example, was a great and accomplished president who recognized that he owed much to his mother. She not only taught young Abe to read, but she went to great lengths to obtain books for him. She wanted to enlarge his world and encourage him to rise above the poverty his family experienced. Lincoln later praised his mother's influence when he said, "All that I am, or hope to be, I owe to my mother."

The Statue of Liberty offers another magnificent example. Each day hundreds of people visit this great statue to gaze upon the beautiful, feminine figure representing the freedom we experience in this great land. Few realize, however, that they are looking at the image of the sculptor's mother! Yes, Frederic Bartholdi chose his own mother as the model for the Statue of Liberty since she represented a heroic and influential person in his life. Now her image lights the way for all who enter New York Harbor.

You and I may not have statues fashioned after us. But as mothers, we have a similar opportunity to light the way for our children—to help shape them and direct them toward becoming all that God created them to be. Like Lady Liberty, we too can stand tall!

A Humbling Realization

Before we get too puffed up, however, we must realize that the ultimate provider for the needs of our children is not us, but God. There are times when we cannot be present to assist our children through a crisis or challenge. But God is there, ever present and always able to supply the help our children need.

I recently learned this lesson firsthand when I went on a "Mom's Weekend Away" with a couple of old high school buddies. Just as we arrived at our hotel, I received a message that my twelve-year-old daughter, Joy, had fallen and dislocated her elbow. She had been rushed to the emergency room of the local hospital by one of our neighbors, and my husband, Curt, had met her there.

"Everything's under control," Curt said over the phone. "You don't need to come home."

Of course, rushing home was my first instinct. I was only forty minutes away, after all. Surely my baby needed me and would not make it through this crisis without me!

My girlfriends didn't allow me to persist in my motherly arrogance for long. Curt could certainly handle the situation, they said; and besides, it might just be good for both him and Joy. Even Joy insisted that I didn't need to come to her rescue.

"Dad's here," she said simply.

I'll be honest. It was difficult for me not to rush to my daughter's side. But I came to the humbling realization that there are times when our kids can and will make it without us—even *should* make it without us. It is tempting as mothers to step in and solve all of our children's problems, thinking we are the only ones who can. The truth is our children need experiences that teach them to cope without us. If we take care of every need and are present in every situation, how will our children learn dependence on God?

Since the accident I've noticed that Joy and her father now share a new and unique bond. Yes, I could have stepped in and tried to save the day, but I would have denied them a wonderful opportunity to work through this challenge together. Sometimes we "wonder-moms" need to humble ourselves and get out of the way!

Rest assured, our influence lingers on whether we are right there with our kids or not. Consider what Thomas Edison, one of America's greatest inventors, had to say about his mother, a wise woman who passed away when Thomas was quite young:

> I did not have my mother long, but she cast over me an influence which has lasted all my life. The good effects of her early training I can never lose. If it had not been for her appreciation and her faith in me at a critical time in my experience, I should never likely have become an inventor. I was always a careless boy,

and with a mother of different mental caliber, I should have turned out badly. But her firmness, her sweetness, her goodness were potent powers to keep me in the right path. My mother was the making of me.[5]

Mothers have one of the most powerful jobs on earth. With God's help, we can influence our children to become world leaders, talented inventors, creative musicians, great athletes, passionate preachers, devoted schoolteachers, committed physicians, and the list goes on. But we must never think pridefully that we are the sole influence in our children's lives! The truth is that while Thomas Edison was greatly influenced by his mother, he somehow made it through most of his life without her. God can use fathers, grandparents, youth leaders, teachers, and friends to assist our children along their journeys. And we should be glad for the assistance!

Someone has said, "God couldn't be everywhere at once, so he created mothers." Not true! God *can* be everywhere at once. He is omnipresent. On the contrary, it is the mother who cannot be there to meet every need and resolve every crisis in her children's lives. Yes, we are highly influential; but let us respectfully and reverently recognize our capabilities and limitations.

God has given each of us the responsibility to train, nurture, develop, prepare, and teach the precious children he has put in our care. Through us—and with his constant guiding presence—he is raising up the next generation. May we be faithful to our high calling! The world may not reward us for our selfless love and diligence. It may never give mothers the credit they are due. But we can still keep going and going—fully assured that one day, in the kingdom that is eternal, we will hear our heavenly Father say, "Well done, good and faithful servant."

POWER POINT

Read: Romans 12. How do these verses encourage you in your role as a mother? Underline or copy the significant verses. Choose one to memorize this week.

Pray: Wonderful Father, thank you for allowing me to participate in the glorious occupation of motherhood. Thank you for being the perfect parent—and the perfect role model! Please help me to remember that my job is significant and eternally important. Help me to glorify you as I work, teach, play, change diapers, and make sandwiches each day. Bless my family with peace and safety as we grow to honor you. In Jesus' name I pray. Amen.

Do: On a large index card, write out your job description. Be creative and include all of your responsibilities. Here's an example:

Investor in Human Resources

Encourages and instructs all clients as to the best use of their time, gifts and talents. Invests love, care, strength, and tears into all clients' accounts. Drives to most locations. Attends all performances and events in which clients are participating. Provides for basic needs of food, clothing, and clean house. Irons occasionally upon request.

Write out Colossians 3:17 on the lower portion of the card, then place the card on your bathroom mirror or in a frame near your kitchen sink. Use it as a constant reminder of your job's significance—and the name of your employer.

The Secret to Your Success
Plugging Into Your Power Source

Of course I'd like to be the ideal mother.
But I'm too busy raising children.
—from the comic strip "The Family Circus" by Bil Keane

Let's be honest. During a typical day in the life of a mother, there are times when it is easy to be a positive person, and there are times when it is not so easy. For me and many of the moms I talk to, the most difficult time to be positive is the hour before dinner. The "killer hour," as many mothers call it, tends to be the time when everyone in the house (including mom) is tired, hungry, and needy. The kids need help with their homework, the baby needs someone to hold her, hubby needs food on the table, and mom needs to figure out some creative way to put together a meal from whatever items happen to be in the pantry or refrigerator. This is the hour that has been known to frazzle even the most positive of moms!

Recently a friend sent me a list of tips on how to be an uplifting wife and mother during the killer hour. Apparently it comes from an old high school home economics book used back in the 1950s. I imagine you will find these guidelines as interesting as I did:

Instructions for Housewives

1. Have dinner ready. Plan ahead, even the night before, to have a delicious meal on the table—on time. This is a way of letting

23

your husband know that you have been thinking about him and are concerned about his needs.

2. Prepare yourself. Take fifteen minutes to rest so you will be refreshed when your husband arrives. Touch up your makeup, put a ribbon in your hair, and be fresh looking. He has just been with a lot of work-weary people. Be a little gay and a little more interesting. His boring day may need a lift.

3. Clear away the clutter. Make one last trip through the main part of the house just before your husband arrives, gathering up schoolbooks, toys, paper, etc. Then run a dustcloth over the tables. Your husband will feel he has reached a haven of rest and order, and it will give you a lift too.

4. Prepare the children. Take a few minutes to wash the children's hands and faces. If they are small, comb their hair, and if necessary, change their clothes. They are little treasures, and he would like to see them playing the part.

5. Minimize the noise. At the time of his arrival, eliminate all noise of washer, dryer, dishwasher, or vacuum. Try to encourage the children to be quiet. Be happy to see him.

6. Some don'ts: Don't greet him with problems or complaints. Don't complain if he's late for dinner. Count this as minor compared with what he might have gone through during the day.

7. Make him comfortable. Have him lean back in a comfortable chair or suggest he lie down in the bedroom. Have a cool or warm drink ready for him. Arrange his pillow and offer to take off his shoes. Speak in a low, soft, soothing, and pleasant voice. Allow him to relax and unwind.

8. Listen to him. You may have a dozen things to tell him, but the moment of his arrival is not the time. Let him talk first.

9. Make the evening his. Never complain if he does not take you out to dinner or to other places of entertainment; instead, try to understand his world of strain and pressure and his need to be home and relax.

10. The goal: Try to make your home a place of peace and order where your husband can feel refreshed.

A few things have changed in our society since the 1950s, don't you agree? It's safe to assume we'd never find these ten tips in a modern textbook! Of course, the "old-fashioned" instructions are not all bad. When I read them to my husband, Curt, he looked at me with a straight face and said, "So what's so funny? I think these tips are great!"

What husband wouldn't like such treatment? (Hey, I'd like someone to do the same for me!) But the reality of life at the beginning of the twenty-first century is that women have new and different responsibilities than they had a half-century ago. Instead of preparing a wonderful, three-course dinner to place on the table at exactly six o'clock, the modern mom spends the killer hour hurrying home through rush-hour traffic after leaving her own job or picking up the kids from soccer practice and ballet lessons. Greeting her husband at the door with a smile is likely to be replaced by a quick hello on the cell phone as she runs off to her PTA meeting and he stops to pick up burgers and fries for the kids.

But while our world has changed in many ways, I believe it is still possible to be a positive wife and mom. We may not follow the ten textbook tips from the 1950s, but we can learn to be affirming parents and spouses no matter what decade we live in.

No Perfect Moms

What expectations do you have for yourself as a mother? Do you want a spotless house? Perfectly mannered kids? A Martha Stewart image? No doubt, you, like me, have a picture in your mind of what a "supermom" looks like. But is your vision realistic or just a glorified picture of what you think you ought to be?

Being a positive mom doesn't mean you have to be a perfect mom. Quite the contrary; the vocabulary of a positive mom generally does not contain the word *perfect*. A positive mom realizes that neither circumstances nor people are ever perfect. She is realistic in her expectations, recognizing that her husband and children have weaknesses as well as strengths. And most importantly, she humbly acknowledges that she has a fair amount of flaws herself.

The truth is we bring to our families a variety of strengths and weaknesses, talents and faults. As Psalm 139:14 reminds us, we are "fearfully and wonderfully made." God knew just what he was doing when he made each one of us—imperfections and all! In fact, he uses our unique combinations of abilities and disabilities to help build loving and balanced homes. Our success as positive mothers begins as we realize that we are glorious creations—a special blend of strengths and shortcomings that God has put together to create a beautiful work of human art, known to our families as "mom."

Often, however, we are tempted to compare ourselves to other women—even to "perfect" television moms—and we forget that God has created us as unique mothers designed with exacting care to benefit our unique homes and families. Personally, I find comfort in the wisdom of an old Chinese proverb: "Nobody's family can hang out the sign, 'Nothing the Matter Here.'" Other families and other mothers may look like they have it all together, but in reality they, like us, have their good points along with their flaws, their challenges, and their regrets.

One of my glaring flaws, for example, is that I am "time impaired." I always seem to be running late. My tardiness is not necessarily the result of selfishness or rudeness, however, but rather a failure to prioritize. I tend to become engrossed in my work, a conversation with a friend, or an activity with my kids, and I simply forget to look at the clock. God has used my family to help me be more time-conscious; they have to be on time to school, practices, and the like, and I'm the one who has to get them there! But God has also used this particular fault to stretch my family, helping them to understand that there are times when a conversation is more important than a schedule. Sometimes we have to be both flexible and forgiving.

Don't be discouraged by your weaknesses; determine instead to build on your strengths. Rejoice that God is at work in your life. He created you. He is developing you. And he is not finished with you yet! Take encouragement from the words of the apostle Paul: "[I am] confident of this, that he who began a good work in you will carry it on to completion until the day of Christ Jesus" (Philippians 1:6).

One Day at a Time

Schedules are one of those areas in which we often compare ourselves to other moms. "Oh, she accomplishes so much!" we hear people say in admiration of a mother who juggles an overwhelming load of responsibilities. But is it realistic to expect that we can we do it all?

It is tempting to think of filling our schedules with a wide assortment of activities and interests. There's so much for a modern woman to do: find a job, take a class, go to the gym, join a service organization, volunteer at the hospital, host a play group—and the list could go on.

But as ironic as it may seem, a positive mom must learn to sometimes give a negative response. In a society offering such myriad opportunities, it is essential that we learn to sometimes say no.

Usually our decision is not a matter of choosing between good activities and bad ones. For the modern mom, there are many wonderful, bright, intriguing, and fulfilling interests to choose from, and all of them are likely to be equally good.

But as Solomon reminds us in Ecclesiastes 3:1, "There is a time for everything, and a season for ever activity under heaven." We don't need to do it all right now! In fact, we must guard against adding too many distractions that will take us away from our main attraction: our relationship with God and our families.

What is on your plate right now? Make a list of all the activities in which you are currently involved. Now add to the list all of your children's activities. (After all, your kids' activities become yours when you drive them to and from practices and classes, attend games and recitals, and volunteer to help out at fund-raisers and concession stands.)

Pretty busy, huh? Is there anything on the list you don't really *have* to be doing? Is there anything on the list you sense God telling you to *stop* doing? You and I must reexamine our activity load on a regular basis, asking ourselves these important questions and making adjustments in our schedules as needed. Although we may think an overflowing plate of activities and interests makes us "well-rounded," the truth is it is more likely to stress us out and make us ineffective in our areas of primary responsibility.

Life always presents us with choices, and some are admittedly hard to make. For many moms it is easier to say yes than it is to say no. But just because you are asked to be president of the women's organization (or the coordinator for the school fund-raiser or the teacher for the five-

Today, I live in the quiet, joyous expectation of good. —Ernest Holmes

year-olds at Vacation Bible School) doesn't mean you must accept. Is it best for your family? Will it use or enhance your gifts and talents? What is the time commitment? Is your husband supportive? Have you prayed about it? These are questions you and I should ask ourselves before saying yes to any new activity.

Ultimately, when it comes to our schedules, we need to follow God's direction and "lean not on [our] own understanding" (Proverbs 3:5). After all, only God knows what the future holds.

When my daughter Joy was in the second grade, I was asked to be a room mother. Of course, I wanted to help out in Joy's class in any way I could, so I immediately said yes. At the time, I was already committed to serve on the school's Board of Trustees and co-lead a large troop of Sonshine Girls (an after-school, character-building club). In addition, my girls were involved in a number of other extracurricular sports and interests that kept me hopping.

Then, shortly after the school year began, I got a call from a publisher asking me to write a book based on a proposal I'd submitted. That was an opportunity I had been waiting for! Suddenly my plate was so full that it was overflowing—and I found myself constantly struggling to keep from making a mess. How did I make it through that year? Only by God's grace. But I'm convinced that if I had just sought his direction back at the beginning of the school year, God—who knew that the book project was around the corner—would have guided me into a less harried, more balanced schedule.

A Personal Mission Statement

One of the greatest gifts we can give our families is to stop rushing down the fast lane and start doing what matters most. And what does matter most? Sometimes we have trouble answering that question because our minds are clouded by the "tyranny of the urgent." We think the most important thing is the thing that's screaming the loudest for our attention. As a result we zoom through life as if it were a sprint race instead of slowing down and relishing it as a meaningful journey.

We can learn a valuable lesson from a recent Special Olympics held in Seattle, Washington. In the 100-meter dash the contestants lined up, ready to run. Then, as the race began, they started out at a slow but steady pace—that is, all except one. Back near the starting line, a young boy with Down Syndrome tripped on the asphalt and fell to the ground. The other runners heard him cry out, and one by one they turned to see what had happened to their friend. Forgetting the race, each one went to the fallen boy's aid. One bent down and kissed the boy's knee and said, "It will be okay." Another helped him to his feet. Then all the contestants joined hands and walked across the finish line together! The crowd cheered for several minutes as they realized they'd just witnessed an amazing demonstration of selfless love.

Is our objective to be the mom who accomplished the most when we come to the end of the race of life? In the rush to get ahead and get things done, are we taking time to love and enjoy the people God has placed in our care? What is our goal in life supposed to be?

I believe each woman must answer these questions personally and individually. We must prayerfully consider the purpose God has given us as mothers. I've found it helpful to actually write a statement of purpose—a mission statement—for my life. This is a declaration of what I believe my life should be about, and it is a helpful guide when I lose my bearings in the midst of the whirlwind around me. Perhaps you will want to write your own mission statement. Here's a sample you can adapt for your purposes:

My Personal Statement of Belief and Purpose

I believe Christ died on the cross for my sins and his Holy Spirit dwells within me, helping me to live according to God's will each day. It is my ultimate goal in life to honor him in all I do.

I believe I was created by God with unique gifts, talents, and abilities that he can use to bless and enrich my family and the people around me.

My strengths include _____.

I recognize that I also have weaknesses that I will try to minimize or overcome with God's help.

I believe my purpose in life is to _____.

My hope for my family is _____.

Your personal statement may read differently, but it should reflect what is truly important to you. When you're finished, share it with your husband and children and ask for their encouragement and accountability.

There are actually several reasons for writing out a life purpose. First, when we know where we are going, we can take the right roads to get there. Without direction we tend to wander aimlessly, doing everything that comes along as society pulls us in many different directions.

Second, a mission statement helps us reflect on what truly matters most in the race of life and helps us to pace ourselves for the long run. "Raising children is not unlike a long-distance race in which the contestants must learn to pace themselves," Christian psychologist Dr. James Dobson says. "That is the secret to winning."[1]

Our personal statement also keeps us focused in a positive direction, helping us live our lives with a clear purpose. "The secret of success is constancy in purpose," Benjamin Disraeli once said.[2] With this written reminder of our beliefs, hopes, and dreams, we are better able to focus our strengths toward our life goals and keep our attention off of our weaknesses.

Plugged Into the Power Source

Cell phones used to be a luxury item; now they seem to be a necessity. It's hard to remember how I ever got by without mine! There's only one thing I hate about them: They have to be connected regularly to a power source in order to be recharged. Many times I've had to make an important call only to see the display on the phone blink "low battery." Cell phones may be a great convenience when they are fully charged, but they are useless if they run out of juice!

The same is true for mothers. Our batteries get drained too. We get tired physically and emotionally from the constant effort to discipline, entertain, and care for our kids. There are days when we feel overwhelmed. Most of us can relate to Erma Bombeck, who said, "When my kids become wild and unruly, I use a nice, safe playpen. When they're finished, I climb out."[3] We all need a break, a respite, a safe haven in which we can reenergize from the cares of motherhood.

Wouldn't it be wonderful if we could plug into an outlet and recharge our battery as easily as we juice up our cell phones? But while we may not be able to recharge electrically, we can spiritually. God's Holy Spirit is our power source, and he is "ever-ready" to meet our needs. The Bible tells us the Holy Spirit helps us in our weaknesses (Romans 8:26). He strengthens and encourages us (Acts 9:31). He leads and guides us (John 16:13). He renews us and replenishes us (Isaiah 32:15). As God's Spirit is at work in our lives, he brings forth wonderful fruit—love, joy, peace, patience, kindness, goodness, faithfulness, gentleness, and self control (Galatians 5:22–23).

Have you plugged into the power source? Has the Holy Spirit

come to dwell in your life? The Bible is quite clear that when we believe in Jesus Christ and trust him for salvation, he places his Holy Spirit within us (Ephesians 1:13–14).

God's plan is simple: It starts with faith in Jesus. John 1:12 says, "Yet to all who received him, to those who believed in his name, he gave the right to become children of God." What about you? Do you have a relationship with your heavenly Father, the Living God? If not, perhaps you would like to take a moment right now to examine the Scriptures (I suggest reading the Gospel of John in a modern Bible translation) and discover for yourself God's beautiful message of salvation—the good news.

What do I mean by good news? The good news is that God loves us. Although none of us is completely good and pure, God—who *is* perfectly good—wants to have a relationship with us. Jesus came to offer his life as the price for our sins so we could be clean and forgiven before God. Now we can have a relationship with the heavenly Father simply by believing that Jesus gave his life for us. We can't work our way into heaven; we can't do enough good deeds to make up for our bad ones. We only have to put our faith in Christ.

Here it is in a nutshell: Out of love for you and me, Jesus came to this earth to die on the cross for our sins. He rose from the dead, giving us hope of eternal life. Now that's good news!

When we are connected with Christ through our faith in him, we are automatically plugged into the power of his Holy Spirit. The Bible says that same great power that brought Jesus back from the grave is at work in the life of every believer (Romans 8:11). That power is flowing from his end; we just need to throw open the switch on ours. We do that by abiding in Christ day by day—by acknowledging his supremacy in our lives, following his leading, and obeying his Word.

When we learn to "plug in" daily, we can begin to experience on a

Commit to the LORD *whatever you do, and your plans will succeed.* —Proverbs 16:3

regular basis the spiritual refreshment that only God can give. We can begin to bear the fruits of "love, joy, peace, patience, kindness, goodness, faithfulness, gentleness and self-control" (Galatians 5:22–23). And that, dear friends, is the *real* secret to our success as positive moms.

POWER POINT

Read: Romans 8 in an easy-to-understand Bible translation. Notice the verses that deal specifically with the Holy Spirit's work in your life. Choose several verses to memorize (I suggest verses 28, 38, and 39).

Pray: Thank you, God, that you have not left me alone to try to live life by myself. Thank you for your Holy Spirit, who lives in me and helps me to be a positive, loving, peaceful, and joyful person each day. Your power—and not my own—is at work in my life, making me the woman you want me to be. Thank you for forgiving my sins and loving me through my weaknesses. Help me to be a positive mom today. In Christ's name, amen.

Do: Prayerfully prepare your own personal mission statement. You may want to refer to the example given earlier in this chapter to help you get started.

Principle #1

THe Pwer OF Encouragement

Therefore encourage one another and build each other up.
—1 Thessalonians 5:11

Few things in the world are more powerful than a positive push.
A smile. A word of optimism and hope.
A "you can do it" when things are tough.
—Richard M. De Vos

Apples of Gold
The Positive Impact of a Good Word

A word aptly spoken is like apples of gold in settings of silver.
—Proverbs 25:11

A number of years ago, a junior high teacher from Minnesota wrote a letter to "Dear Abby" telling the story of a remarkable life lesson she learned from her students. She began by describing a difficult day in her math class when the kids were particularly cranky with one another and discouraged about the lesson. Frustrated, the teacher told the class to put away their math books and place one sheet of blank paper on their desks. She then instructed them to list the names of their classmates along the left-hand side of the page and write next to each name the nicest thing they could think of to say about each person. The impromptu exercise helped, because as the students turned in their assignments, the teacher noticed that everyone was a little more relaxed and at ease.

Over that weekend, the teacher took the time to write each student's name on a blank page and painstakingly copied the kind thoughts that were expressed about each of the kids. On Monday morning, she handed the students their lists. The room was abuzz with whispers and comments such as, "Wow, really?" "I didn't know anyone liked me that much!" "I never knew that meant anything to anyone."

Then the assignment was put away, and class continued with the students feeling better about themselves and each other.

Years later, the math teacher attended the untimely funeral of one of her students who was killed while serving his country in Vietnam. After the service, the parents of this brave young man approached the teacher and said, "We want to show you something Mark was carrying when he was killed." The father pulled a crumpled piece of paper from his wallet, and as he unfolded it, the teacher recognized her handwriting. It was the paper from that long-ago assignment consisting of all the nice things the young man's classmates had said about him! The parents thanked the teacher, saying that their son had always treasured the encouraging words.

Other former students standing nearby spoke up. One smiled sheepishly, saying he kept his list of compliments in his top desk drawer at home. Another said his sheet had been placed in his wedding album. A third person pulled out his wallet and proudly displayed his folded page as if it were a prized possession. Overwhelmed, the teacher sat down and cried, realizing the full value of that impromptu assignment and the power of encouraging words.

Abby responded to the teacher's letter in her column with a quote from George Herbert: "Good words are worth much and cost little."[1]

There is no greater investment we can make in the lives of our children than giving them generous doses of encouraging words. It costs us so little in time and effort, but the rewards are priceless. When our young people are reminded of their God-given value, they receive deposits of confidence, security, and well-being in their emotional bank accounts. They begin building on their strengths, knowing they have something to contribute to this world. On the other hand, when our children have nothing positive to believe about themselves, their emotional bank accounts can become bankrupt—overdrawn by the negative comments and disappointments that occur every day in the world around them.

The old adage "Sticks and stones can break my bones but words will never hurt me" is certainly *not* true. Think back to when you were a child. Do you remember a taunt or jeer you received from other kids at some point in your growing-up years? Most of us can! No matter how small or insignificant the comment was, the hurt can still linger in our memories. Isn't it amazing that we still remember these incidents, even though many years have come and gone?

Some psychologists say that for every negative comment a person receives, they need to hear ten positive comments to overcome the effects of the negative one. Ten to one—now that's a lot of positive words, especially when you consider all the negative input our kids are likely to encounter during a typical day.

It is easy for any child to become a target for cruel words in today's society. Kids ridicule each other for everything from physical features to clothes to being a "goody-goody." The adolescent years can be especially difficult with its added pressure on young teens to "fit in" and belong to a group. Many of the school shootings reported in the national media in recent years were carried out by kids who were ridiculed by their classmates or treated like outcasts. The hurt that comes from being mocked or ostracized can leave an indelible imprint on a child's impressionable mind.

Even a caring family member, youth leader, or teacher can make a careless statement and unknowingly hurt a child. What may seem to an adult like a slight or simple comment can loom large to a young person. I remember an incident my daughter Grace experienced when she was five years old. Grace is a lovely young lady, and she is blessed with a good many freckles on her face. One day at church, a well-meaning adult commented on her appearance and concluded, "Your nickname should be 'Freckles'!" What seemed like a quaint observation to the woman crushed Grace, who had not realized that her freckles were so noticeable to others. It actually took many more than ten positive comments from mom to overcome this one negative comment that had unintentionally hurt Grace's feelings.

Reckless words and unkind criticism are like a highway demolition crew in our children's hearts. They have the potential to cause great damage and make for a rocky road in life. But as mothers, we have the responsibility and the privilege of filling in the potholes. Do the math. If our kids encounter just two negative comments or put-downs during the course of the day, they need approximately twenty fillings of love and appreciation to plug up the potholes.

How many times during a typical day do you build your child up with encouraging words? Two, maybe three times? Some days, that may not be enough! We need to be deliberate about building up our children's strengths and putting regular deposits in their emotional bank accounts. We need to make sure they're getting a positive picture of who they are.

Not that our children's sense of self-worth should be dependent on the affirmation we give them. This is an important concept to understand and pass on. Our children's self-worth, like our own, must be based on the fact that God made us and loves us. Every person has value as a beautiful and miraculous creation of their heavenly Father. We affirm our kids—and others—not because they are dependent on praise, but because our encouragement can provide them with the strength they need to press on to reach their full potential. In fact, the word *encourage* means "to put courage into, to give strength." We have the responsibility each day to give strength and courage to our children to help them face life's opportunities and challenges.

As part of that process, we need to teach our kids that they are valuable no matter what comments are made about them, good or bad. "If God is for us, who can be against us?" Paul writes in Romans 8:31. From an early age, children need to establish in their hearts and minds that their worth is not wrapped up in what they do or what anyone else thinks about what they do; rather, it is based on who they are in Christ.

Consider the analogy of a luxury car and the fuel we put into it to make it run. The positive affirmation we give our children is the gasoline we put in the tank of their car. The car has value whether we put gas in the tank or not; but if we want the car to go somewhere and stay in good condition, we need to fill it up with quality fuel. Our kids have great value. The more we fill them with the fuel of encouragement, the more energy they will have to reach their goals and follow their dreams.

Are you filling your kids with quality, high-octane fuel? Proverbs 12:25 says, "An anxious heart weighs a man down, but a kind word cheers him up." Our kind words and encouragement have a powerful effect in our children's lives. They're some of the most effective tools available for positive moms.

Be on the Lookout!

Sometimes my kids must think I have an invisible magnifying glass that focuses in on everything they do wrong. I can't blame them. There are definitely days when it seems I'm constantly finding something to correct in their actions or conversation. I'm not totally out of line, of course; it *is* my job as a parent to discipline, train, and help my kids grow into well-behaved young adults.

Most moms, I think, are like me—fairly adept at discovering their children's faults. Somehow it's easier for us to find and focus on our kids' mistakes than it is to be attentive to what they are doing right. But our challenge as positive moms is to identify our children's positive attributes and actions and encourage them in those things.

Unfortunately, no one has invented a magnifying glass powerful enough to uncover the good in our children. We have to make our own observations—and some days that can be difficult!

In the summer of 1998, our family had an exciting opportunity to go to London for a business conference. Imagine our delight when, several months before the trip, my husband decided we should take an extra week to see Paris as well! To prepare for our journey, I immediately began teaching Grace and Joy about the French culture and language. We learned about key points of interest such as the Eiffel Tower, the Arc de Triomphe, the Louvre, the palace at Versailles, and more.

The Eiffel Tower seemed to capture the girls' imagination the most, and as our plane touched down in the French capital, they pressed their noses to the window to search for the famous landmark. Sure enough, they found it! During the taxi drive to the hotel, they found it again. Then they found it from our hotel window. In fact, every place we went in Paris and the surrounding areas, they were on the lookout for the Eiffel Tower—and they found it every time!

Why were they able to find it? Because they were looking for it! We too can find the good qualities in our children. They'll pop out at us from nearly every vantage point if we'll just be on the lookout for them.

What are the Eiffel Towers in our children's lives? We need to be on the lookout for qualities such as kindness, gentleness, joyfulness, gratitude, self-control, patience—attributes the Bible calls "fruit of the Spirit" (see Galatians 5:22–23). We should notice and encourage these qualities as we see them begin to sprout in our children's words and actions. Unique talents and abilities (a good singing voice, a skill in soccer, a mind for math, a way with words, an artistic flair, etc.) offer additional opportunities to encourage our kids to reach for their highest potential. We must simply be determined to find these points of praise! Just as my daughters were bent on finding the Eiffel Tower from every location in Paris, we can be on the lookout for our children's positive gifts and attributes in everything they do from day to day.

How do we identify these pillars of positive potential? We begin by paying attention to our children's interests. Do they enjoy drawing? Odds are we will find an opportunity to give a sincere compliment as we observe their finished artwork or watch them create a new masterpiece. Do they like to swim? We need to take a moment to watch them paddle in the pool and verbally admire their skill. The key is making ourselves available to our kids. How can we comment on a soccer game we didn't see? Or praise a poem we didn't take the time to read? To be positive moms, we need to spend *quantity* as well as *quality* time with our children.

Secondly, until encouragement becomes habit, we need to remind ourselves to fill up our children's emotional fuel tanks with accolades. Unfortunately, our kids don't come with an "affirmation gauge" like the gas gauge in our cars. We don't necessarily get a warning that lets us know they're almost on "empty." We need to stay constantly on the lookout for good and admirable qualities so we can seize the moment and offer encouragement when an opportunity arises.

While shopping recently, I found a pillbox in the shape of the Eiffel Tower. The price was fair, so I purchased it and set it on a bookshelf in my study. Now it serves as a daily reminder to diligently and deliberately search for the good qualities in my daughters and find opportunities to strengthen them through my words. What will help you remember to encourage your kids? Perhaps you can purchase several inexpensive magnifying glasses at a local drugstore and attach a note to the glasses saying, "Have you searched for the good in your child today?" Then you can place the magnifying glasses in strategic places you're sure to see, such as by your purse or in the pantry or in the car. Or you might draw a little gauge on an index card and write yourself a note saying, "Have you put fuel in your kid's emotional tank today?"

I have yet to find the man, however exalted his station, who did not do better work and put forth greater effort under a spirit of approval than under a spirit of criticism. —Charles Schwab

43

Experts say the best way to form a new habit is to deliberately do the action for at least twenty-one consecutive days. Why not begin now to form the habit of speaking positive words to your children? Set a goal of saying at least three encouraging comments to each child each day. As you put them to bed at night, check to see if you have put enough verbal deposits in their emotional bank accounts that day. If you come up short, you can use this bedside time to make up the difference before they doze off.

Be deliberate and persistent for three weeks. Look for those opportune times when you have a quiet moment or two with your child. Besides bedtime, I find the two best times for me to compliment and encourage my daughters are when I take them to school and when I pick them up in the afternoon. It's easy for me to think of good things to say about them as I send them off in the morning, and I can usually find areas for encouragement in our afternoon review of the day's events.

We need to practice this "attitude of accolades" in order to make affirmation and encouragement natural parts of our daily conversation. But the best practice is not done with our kids, our spouse, or any other person. The best practice is to begin each day by praising our heavenly Father. We should, after all, adore him first and foremost in our lives. "I will praise the LORD all my life, I will sing praise to my God as long as I live," the psalmist wrote in Psalm 146:2. As we focus on the praiseworthy qualities of Almighty God and form the habit of praising him, we can't help but become more positive and encouraging—and more likely to have positive comments on the tips of our tongues for our children and others.

Giving Strength through Our Words

When it comes to strengthening and encouraging our kids, there are four guidelines that can help our words have greater power and effectiveness.

1. Be Specific

"You're terrific!" "Wow, you did great!" "Super job!" These are uplifting sentiments that can encourage and inspire our children, and our kids certainly benefit from hearing them. Brief, general phrases like these have their time and their purpose. But if we truly want to give a special gift to our children, we need to offer them specific compliments. Instead of broad statements that could fit almost anyone doing almost anything, "personalized praise" lets our kids know we're really paying attention.

"I think you are a terrific goalie. Very few soccer goalies can stop the side kicks like you can." "I loved the way you painted that picture. You really have an eye for color!" By using specifics, we not only give our children a wonderful gift, we add a beautiful bow and a card that says, "This compliment is meant for you, and only you." Children recognize our sincerity when we use specific details to describe the qualities we appreciate about them.

2. Be Prepared

It may seem insincere to prepare positive comments in advance, but preparation doesn't undermine the sincerity we want to convey to our kids. A public speaker is not deemed insincere simply because she has planned out what she is going to say beforehand. Quite the contrary; she is able to deliver a much better, more thoughtful address when she puts her thoughts together in advance.

The same is true for moms and positive comments. It never hurts to be prepared! If we know we will be attending our daughter's piano recital, for example, we can think of some specific compliments that will fit the situation. "Honey, I am so proud of you," we might say. "It takes a lot of courage to play in front an audience, and you did so well. I especially liked…"

Here are some other comments we can have ready to use when the time and place is right:

- "I love spending time with you. You are a bright spot in my day."

- "I'll never forget the day you were born. You were so beautiful, and you still are."

- "God made you special, and I am so glad he made you a part of this family."

- "You gave it your best effort. That makes me proud of you. You are a hard worker."

- "Your hugs are so special. Can I have one right now?"

- "You did a fantastic job! Your hard work and preparation paid off!"

- "I love the way you _____. I can tell God has given you a special talent."

- "Thank you for _____. You bring joy to our family."

- "I appreciate the way you _____. You are a very thoughtful person."

3. Be Creative

It is helpful to use a variety of ways to express affirmation and encouragement to your family members. Variety is the spice of life, they say—even when it comes to speaking positive words.

Several years ago, the Camp Fire Boys and Girls declared a national "Absolutely Incredible Kid Day." Recognizing the value of affirmative words to children, the organization encouraged parents, teachers, and youth workers to get creative and write special notes of appreciation and praise to the kids in their care. The goal of the Camp Fire effort was to get adults to begin raving about their children's assets—and to promote the best qualities of the next generation.

We don't need a national holiday to write special notes to our children. We can pen a sentence or two on a sticky pad or note card and leave it:

- On their pillow

- In their lunch box

- In their shoes

- On the door to their room

- In their backpack

- Between the pages of a textbook or their Bible

- On the bathroom mirror

For more variety, try e-mailing a note to your child or sending a card through the mail. (It's always fun to receive a letter in the mailbox.) Or write a few sentences of encouragement, fold the paper into a small box, and wrap the box with fancy paper and a bow. Then present the gift at a special moment.

If you want to get even more creative, make an audio or videotape expressing your appreciation for your child. (You can bet that tape will be played over and over again!) If you have a poetic bent, write a poem or song. Or use the letters in your child's name to make an acronym, with each letter standing for some positive trait you see. Then add artwork (if you can) and frame the page.

4. Be Resourceful

There are many good resources that can serve as catalysts for our positive words. Bible verses can be particularly effective in offering godly compliments and building on eternal qualities such as love, joy, and peace. I'll never forget the letter I got from my boyfriend Curt (now my husband!) the summer I served as a camp counselor in East Texas. He quoted from Proverbs 31:29: "Many women do noble things, but you surpass them all." Wow! I walked a little taller that day, knowing that Curt cared enough to compliment me with such a meaningful verse!

We can use Scripture to encourage our children as well. We can compliment them on demonstrating the same kind of loyalty that Ruth showed toward Naomi or being a good friend like Jonathan was to David. Quoting from Psalm 139:13–16, we can assure them that God designed them to be unique and special. Turning to Proverbs 1:7, we can let them know they show wisdom when they reverence the Lord. As we read the Beatitudes from the Sermon on the Mount, we can tell our kids that we see in them a pure heart or a hunger and thirst for righteousness. From 1 Corinthians 13 we can point out the qualities of love we see in their words and actions.

Reading books or watching television or movies with our children can be resources too—offering both good examples for comparison and bad examples for contrast. For instance, as we read *Little House on the Prairie* by Laura Ingalls Wilder or watch reruns of the old television show, we can point out Laura's respect for her parents and say, "I'm grateful that you have the same kind of respect for your dad and me that Laura seems to have for her parents." Later, as we read Mark Twain's *Tom Sawyer* or watch one of the movies adapted from the book, we can point out the heartache that Tom's troublemaking caused Aunt Polly and say, "I'm certainly thankful for the way you behave. Your obedience is a blessing to me." After a comment like that from mom, a child is not going to want to run toward mischief anytime soon!

The Right Kind of Attention

A number of years ago a peculiar man decided to dress up in a silly-looking red Spiderman suit, attach suction cups to his hands and feet, and climb up the side of one of the tallest buildings in the world. When he reached the top, 125 stories up, the crowd that had gathered below broke out in thunderous applause. Both the police and news reporters were on the roof ready to greet the self-made superhero.

"Why did you do it?" they asked.

His reply was simple: "I love to hear the applause."[2]

A man risks his life in a pair of red pajamas—just to hear the applause of people! It is amazing the lengths we will go to receive encouragement and praise. But as William James once said, "The deepest craving of human nature is the need to feel appreciated."[3]

Children are no exception. In fact, I'm convinced kids are born with an invisible sign around their necks that says, "I want to feel important." Too often, however, they must struggle to gain the attention and praise they need from the important people in their lives. Schoolteachers know that children who do not seem to get enough attention for doing the right things are the ones who tend to act up. In the kids' minds, negative attention is better than no attention.

As mothers, we hold the key. There is no better stimulus to motivate young people toward goodness than the knowledge that their best qualities are noticed and appreciated by mom.

Several years ago a friend and I went out to lunch at a delightful little tearoom. It was a popular restaurant and quite crowded during the lunch hour. As we waited in line to be seated, we noticed the people in front of us were rude and impatient with the hostess. So when our turn came to be seated, we were extra-kind to the woman, knowing that she was having a difficult day.

A few moments after we settled in at our table, the hostess returned with a tray of glasses filled with ice water. Among the assortment of plain glasses were two crystal goblets. She took the plain glasses to a nearby table then brought the expensive goblets to us. "You two were nice to me today," she said, "so I brought you the nicest glasses we have in the restaurant. Thank you for your kindness."

Imagine how we felt! Our kind words had seemed so small and insignificant, yet this woman had noticed them. And since we'd made her feel special, she decided to make us feel special. Now, do you think we were going to complain about the food or rush our waitress that day? Not on your life! Our kindness had been rewarded, and we were happy to continue in it.

Our kids will respond the same way when we deliver a compliment to them on a silver platter. They will want to keep up the good work!

Lavina Christensen Fugal, the 1995 Mother of the Year, offers mothers the following advice: "Love your children with all your hearts.... Praise them for important things.... Praise them a lot. They live on it like bread and butter."[4] A few simple words of affirmation and admiration may be just the spark our kids need to try harder and pursue greater dreams. Let's continue to dish out delicious morsels of encouraging words and watch our children's finest qualities strengthen and grow!

POWER POINT

Read: Ephesians 4:29–32; Colossians 3:12–15; and Philippians 4:8. How do these verses help you to become a better encourager to your children? Underline or write out a verse that is especially meaningful.

♡ Pray: Wonderful heavenly Father, I praise you for your omnipotent wisdom in creation. I thank you that each and every person was created by design, with flaws and weaknesses as well as strengths and talents. Help me to accentuate the positive with my kids. Help me to see their potential and encourage their best qualities. Help me to be a builder of my family with the words of my mouth, speaking praise for the good things I see in my spouse and children.

☺ Do: Write out four specific accolades for each of your family members and deliver one of them each week for the next four weeks. When you see the positive response you get, you may want to make one day a week your note-writing day to regularly express to your family members and friends how special they are.

Great Expectations
Helping Your Children Discover Their Potential

*"For I know the plans I have for you," declares the LORD, "plans
to prosper you and not to harm you, plans to give you hope and
a future. Then you will call upon me and come and pray to me,
and I will listen to you. You will seek me and find me when you
seek me with all your heart."*
—Jeremiah 29:11–13

Imagine a beautiful sailboat with large, billowing sails, moving across the surface of the wide, blue-green ocean. Strong gusts of wind blow into the sails, filling the broad canvases and propelling the vessel to new and different places—far beyond any port it has ever known.

As mothers, our affirming influence is like that breeze that firmly sends the sailboat of our children's lives across the waters of life. Helping our children reach their destination—to achieve the fullness of their God-given potential—is one of the most rewarding aspects of our job as moms. But we must be careful. It is tempting to impose our own expectations on our children, to try to push them in the direction we want for them rather than the direction God has planned for them since the beginning of time. Our challenge is to learn how to be the wind in their sails without blowing them off the course God has set for their lives.

Olympic swimmer Summer Sanders believes that "champions are raised, not born." In her book by that title, she notes that good parenting can be the key factor in making the experiences of a child's life positive and empowering. Sanders, who swam her way to two gold medals, one silver medal, and one bronze medal in the 1992 Olympics, believes that her parents played a big role in helping her get to that level of world competition. Her mom and dad did not push her or drive her to her success, she says; they simply provided joyful support, positive encouragement, and constant reassurance that they were there for her whether she won or lost. Summer believes her parents gave her what few men and women ever receive: "the infinite satisfaction and self-confidence that comes from getting to do what you do best and knowing you're tapping your potential to the fullest."[1]

How do you unlock the door to *your* child's potential in a healthy and affirming way? The Bible gives us the key when it tells us to "train a child in the way he should go" (Proverbs 22:6). A better translation might be "train a child *according to his bent.*" In other words, our children have been put together by God in a unique way and pointed by him in a unique direction. Our job is to recognize that direction, then encourage and instruct our kids to grow and develop in their God-given way.

In the field of education, we can apply this idea to identify our children's unique learning styles (whether auditory, visual, or kinesthetic). In the area of personalities, we can learn to deal with each child according to his or her particular temperament (whether choleric, sanguine, melancholy, or phlegmatic). When it comes to skills and talents, we can steer our children toward the activities for which they seem to have an aptitude (sports, music, art, drama, academics, and so on.)

Study Your Children Well

Our children are not exactly like anyone else—not us, not our spouse, not their siblings. They are not clones of the other kids in the school or neighborhood. We may see similarities between them and others in appearance, in temperament, or in aptitude; but our children are unique individuals with their own incredible boatloads of potential and possibilities.

Under my own roof dwell four completely peerless individuals (and two rather unique dogs). Each person in our home represents a one-of-a-kind product of the Creator. My husband, Curt, is a confident, hard-working, highly driven businessman. He has a multitude of hobbies and interests ranging from golf to antique shopping. He rarely sits still.

Grace, our fourteen-year-old, is a delightful and bubbly sanguine who loves to sing, act, shop, and decorate. She is involved in a youth group at a large church in our area and enjoys every opportunity to get together with her sweet and equally energetic friends.

Twelve-year-old Joy, meanwhile, relates best to the small youth group at our home church. She has wonderful friends, but she enjoys being at home as much as being with other kids. She is an excellent student and a talented gymnast. She is also kind, thoughtful, and gentle.

Then there is me, Mom. You could characterize me as one of those "creative types." It is easy and enjoyable for me to spend hours at the computer writing ideas for a speech, article, or book. I love to be with my friends, but I also value time alone. Teaching and hospitality are my gifts, so our house is usually buzzing with people and parties.

Clearly God made each one of my family members in a special way, creating a beautiful collage of personalities for our unique home. He has also given my daughters different interests, abilities, and temperaments. Already I can see him leading the girls down separate paths, with a definite plan and a purpose for their individual lives.

Take a moment to think about the unique qualities of your own family members. How would you describe each of your children? To be positive moms, we need to be students of our kids. That may sound funny since we tend to view ourselves as teachers of our children and

If one advances confidently in the direction of his dreams and endeavors to love the life which he has imagined, he will meet with a success unexpected in common hours. —Henry David Thoreau

not the other way around. But in order to help them grow and mature to their fullest potential, we must get to know our children, understand them, and recognize their strengths and weaknesses. We must help them discover their unique bents. Then, once they are pointed in the direction God has set for them, we can be the wind in their sails, helping them reach the destination of their own special goals and dreams.

Step #1: See the Potential

In 1882 a precious, nineteen-month-old girl lost her sight and hearing due to an unfortunate illness. As she grew up she became wild and unruly, with seemingly little opportunity to make something of herself. Most people would have looked at her situation in life and given up on her. But one teacher dared to look beyond the surface of her disabilities and see the potential inside of her.

Anne Sullivan, though nearly blind herself, began teaching little Helen Keller how to read, write, and communicate in what seemed to Helen a foreign language. Eventually Helen attended Radcliffe College, where she studied French and Greek and learned to type her papers and assignments using a typewriter with Braille keys. At the age of twenty-one, Helen published her life story and became a well-known public figure. She was compassionate toward the needs of others and maintained an excitement about life that many people who can see and hear never possess.

Living in a dark and silent world did not keep Helen Keller from reaching her God-given potential—mainly because one woman, Anne Sullivan, made the effort to look beyond the limitations and imagine what God could do with the abilities he had given to her young student. How about you? Do you see the abundant potential that your child possesses? Many times our children's worst attributes glare at us. We're so focused on what our children *can't* do that we fail to see what they *can* do. Yet each child is born with certain abilities and gifts to offer to the world. We need to identify these things and build on them. As Helen Keller said, "I thank God for my handicaps, for through them, I have found myself, my work and my God."[2]

Exploring the possibilities, gifts, and treasures within our children can be a wonderful journey of discovery. How do you begin? Start by writing down the potential you see in your children in four key areas of growth: mental, physical, spiritual, and social. The Bible tells us that Jesus developed in each of these areas throughout his boyhood: "And Jesus grew in wisdom and stature, and in favor with God and men" (Luke 2:52). Are your children academically inclined? Do they excel in a particular subject? What physical skills or attributes do they possess? How are they developing in their relationship with God? Are they comfortable around adults? Are they good at making friends?

Examine and observe each of your children, noting those qualities, interests, or aptitudes you see God developing in their lives. Pray over those things as you write them down, asking God to help you understand how they can be developed and used. Share with your children the possibilities you see for their lives. Offer them a vision of their God-given potential.

Be careful, though, not to make your kids feel trapped by your personal wishes or expectations for them. An interest in science may lead your son to become a high school chemistry teacher, not a brain surgeon. An aptitude for the piano may offer your daughter a lifelong outlet for relaxation and pleasure, not a career at Carnegie Hall. Our task is to encourage them in their bent—not to plan out the details.

Step #2: Offer Opportunities for Growth

As your children grow up, it's a good idea to let them try their hand at a variety of things—sports, dance, art, music, and the like. I'm not suggesting, however, that you overload them with organized activities. A heavy schedule of classes, practices, and meetings can lead to burnout— both for the kids and for the frazzled mom-turned-chauffeur. Instead allow your children to test different areas of interest by practicing at home with family and friends first. A bent for art may show up as your son sketches "doggies" or paints flowers on scrap paper at the kitchen table. A skill for soccer may become evident as your daughter kicks a ball around the backyard with the neighborhood kids. As a particular interest or aptitude emerges, you can look for a class or team or meeting where they can develop that skill or talent further.

But don't be in a rush! Today's culture places an unspoken pressure on parents to engage their children in organized activities from a very early age. Our fear is that our children will be left behind if we hold them back while every other kid in the universe starts the activity in preschool. That concern is unfounded, however. In many cases our children will excel in an area at a later age because they've developed a love for the activity and have a natural skill, while kids who were pushed at an early age lose interest and don't progress.

In fact, many great athletes started their sport during adolescence or later. Consider these Olympic examples just for starters:

- Crissy Ahmann, who won a gold and a silver medal swimming in the 1992 Olympics, took up the sport in her college years.

- Matt Biondi, one of the most decorated male Olympic swimmers, favored basketball over pool sports until about age fifteen.

- Justin Huish, winner of the gold medal in archery in 1996, didn't shoot an Olympic-style bow until he was fourteen.

- Bonnie Blair, the world's fastest woman speed skater, grew up being competitive in many sports, including cycling, track, and gymnastics. She was twelve before she realized she wanted to skate more than anything else.[3]

Yes, it's good for us to encourage our children to do their best. But we must also allow them to grow and develop at their own God-given pace.

Step #3: Set Realistic Goals

Can you imagine sitting in an airplane when the pilot makes this announcement over the intercom? "I have some good news and some bad news," he says. "The bad news is we have lost one engine, along with our direction finder. The good news is we have a tailwind, and wherever we are headed, we are getting there at 650 miles per hour!"

Personally, I don't think I'd like to be on a flight headed fast to who-knows-where. And we don't want to send our kids skipping through life without direction, preparation, or purpose either. They need goals—targets to shoot for—as well as strategies for reaching them.

As a former track coach, I used to teach young athletes two important principles: Run your best and keep your eyes on the finish line. The Bible tells us to do the same on the track of life. "Let us run with perseverance the race marked out for us," Hebrews 12:1–2 says. "Let us fix our eyes on Jesus, the author and perfecter of our faith." As we keep our eyes focused on the goal of serving Christ and becoming more like him, we are less distracted in our race by the cares, frustrations, and temptations of the world. Having Jesus as our first and foremost goal keeps us on the right track!

"Goals give you the specific direction to make your dreams come true," says Bob Conklin.[4] This is as important for children as it is for adults. After setting Jesus as their first goal, you can set other goals with your kids on an annual basis once they're mature enough to understand the concept (usually by about eight years old).

Set aside a time each year when you will work with each child to develop his or her specific goals for the next twelve months. My dad taught my sister and me to write out our annual goals every New Year's Day. I've continued this habit throughout my life and have encouraged my daughters to do the same. It is a good idea to write down one goal for each of the four growth areas mentioned earlier—mental, physical, spiritual, and social. Keep in mind that these goals should be realistic, obtainable, yet stretching. They should not be *your* goals for your children; rather, they should be an expression of their goals for themselves.

The goals should also be measurable. "To be a better basketball player" is a nice idea, but it's not something that can be measured objectively. A better goal is something like "I will put the ball up and shoot at least five times in every game." Or "I will score at least thirty points for my team this season." Sometimes it's good to set a minimum and a maximum goal, with the first one being fairly easy to achieve and the second one requiring a greater stretch.

As you work together with your children to plan their goals for the year, talk to them about strategies they could use to reach the desired goals. For instance, if your child has set the "mental" goal of reading two new books per month (in addition to school requirements), you may want to jot down a strategy for accomplishing that feat. Perhaps he or she can read for thirty minutes each afternoon after school and an hour every Saturday.

As your children get older, consider helping them develop a "five-year plan" in which they set a bigger, general goal of where they want to be in five years and talk about how they plan to get there. If your son wants to go to college, what courses must he take in high school—and how good must his grades be? If your daughter wants to draw closer to

Train a child in the way he should go, and when he is old he will not turn from it. —Proverbs 22:6

the Lord, what disciplines of prayer, Bible study, and service does she need to develop?

But even as you set goals with your kids, remember: Change happens. Be open to new possibilities, and help your children understand that the circumstances of life may put a twist in their plans. The important thing is that they adjust to whatever God allows in their lives and look for ways to set new goals in different directions. Case in point: Joni Eareckson Tada was an active teenager who had a wonderful outlook on life and high hopes for the future. But God had other plans for her life, and when an accident left her paralyzed below the neck, she adjusted her goals accordingly. Today she is a wonderfully accomplished artist and author and an inspiration to everyone who knows her.

Because we don't know what the future holds, we must always view our goals with our eyes fixed first on Jesus. Whatever life brings, however our goals change, we can hold on to the assurance that God is at work in our lives "to will and to act according to his good purpose" (Philippians 2:13).

Step #4: Support Their Endeavors

Sometime ago Dr. Donald Clifton of SRI/Gallup Poll conducted a study to see if there was a correlation between an athlete's performance and the presence of family members in the audience. The evidence showed that those athletes who had moms and other family members watching from the sidelines were more likely to perform at a higher level than those who had no one cheering them on.[5]

During my junior year in college, I decided to run a marathon. After months of diligent training for this twenty-six-mile test of endurance, the day of the race finally arrived. My entire family and several friends showed up to cheer me on. My mother actually made signs with encouraging messages—for example, "I can do everything through him who gives me strength" (Philippians 4:13)—and she and the others held them up for me to see at strategic spots along the course. My father and my boyfriend (now my husband, Curt) even jumped into the race and ran a few miles with me just to encourage me.

As you can imagine, it was a grand and glorious moment when I crossed the finish line! Who can say how well I might have fared without the support of my loved ones? I know without a doubt that I gave it my very best because my family and friends were there.

As positive moms, we can support our children by being there—by taking them to their lessons and practices and showing up for their recitals and games. We can encourage them by looking for opportunities to build up their self-confidence and skills. A little research on our part can help. What skills are involved in your child's field of interest? Does your city or county have a league? Are there classes in that skill for his or her age group? Who are the best teachers or coaches? Is the teacher qualified and able to motivate and work well with kids?

Of course, our children will not always succeed at what they do. We need to be there when they win—and also when they lose. Through the tears, heartaches, and disappointments, we need to lend a listening ear and a shoulder to cry on. Our children should know that we are a safe haven for them—that we will love them whether they perform perfectly or mess up. Our support must be unconditional!

We are not lowering our expectations by comforting our children rather than scolding them when they don't perform to the best of their abilities. Everyone has a bad day or an off performance. By our response to their failure, we can either douse their confidence or be the catalyst that helps them want to try harder next time. They may fall, but they'll dig deep for the courage to get up if they know mom is there saying, "I believe in you!"

The apostle Paul said it best: "Brothers, I do not consider myself yet to have taken hold of it. But one thing I do: Forgetting what is behind and straining toward what is ahead, I press on toward the goal to win the prize for which God has called me heavenward in Christ Jesus" (Philippians 3:13–14). What great words for us to pass on to our children! We can say to them, "I know you are not there yet, but you will be. Let's forget what is behind us and press forward to reach the goal God intends for you!"

The Blessing of Encouragement

The story is told of an elderly man who once approached the famous nineteenth-century poet and artist Dante Gabriel Rossetti. Under his arm, the old man carried a number of sketches and drawings he'd recently completed. He asked the great artist to look at his work and tell him if they showed any degree of artistic value or skill.

Rossetti looked over the drawings carefully for a few minutes before concluding that they did not show the least sign of artistic talent. Gently he broke the news to the old man, who seemed disappointed but not surprised.

The man then asked Rossetti to look at just a few more drawings done by a younger art student. Rossetti agreed, and this time he found the work to be quite good. With enthusiasm, he told the old man that this young student showed great potential and should be encouraged to pursue a career as an artist.

The man seemed deeply moved by these words, so Rossetti asked if the drawings were perhaps the work of his son. "No," the man replied sadly. "These are mine also, done forty years ago. If only I had heard your praise then! For you see, I got discouraged and gave up too soon."

Perhaps this unknown artist would be a household name today if someone had taken him under wing and encouraged him to continue to hone his skills and pursue his dream. As a young man, he did not get the affirmation and blessing he needed at a critical time in his life. As positive moms, we can help ensure that our children do not suffer the same fate.

Many books have been written about the importance of parental blessings in a young person's life. Blessings are not a new idea; the great patriarchs of the Bible often spoke blessings to their children, thereby helping to mold and shape their futures. How can you bless your kids? Begin by telling them that God created them unique and special, and he has a great plan for their lives. Read Jeremiah 29:11–13 and Psalm 139:14–16 to them. Pray with them, asking God to bless the good qualities you see in them and to guard and guide them as they go forward with their lives.

Our children are embarking on an exciting adventure. Who knows what the future holds for them? Only God—the one who has built their boat, charted their course, and who now gives us the privilege of being wind in their sails. As positive moms, may our affirmation, encouragement, and unconditional love help them reach their destination!

POWER POINT

Read: The exciting story of Esther in the book of the Bible by that name. Reflect on the potential that Mordecai saw in Esther and what he did to encourage and support her. Notice how God used her life for an important purpose as a result of a pursued dream.

Pray: I praise you, Lord, for having a plan and a purpose for each one of us. You love us, and you know more about us than we know about ourselves. Help me as a mother to see the potential and the possibilities in each of my children. Help me to be faithful to support them in the direction of their bent. Help me to refrain from placing any selfish or unrealistic expectations on them. Help us to set realistic and wise goals and to keep our focus on those goals. Most importantly, help us to keep our eyes fixed on you, the author and finisher of our faith.

☺ **Do:** Write down the positive qualities and attributes you see in your children in the four key areas of growth: mental, physical, spiritual, and social. Plan a time to sit down with each child (age eight and up) individually and set realistic goals for growth in these areas. Pray with your children as they go to bed at night, asking God to bless the specific plans he has for each one of them.

The Beauty of a Smile
Bringing Son-shine to Others

What sunshine is to flowers, smiles are to humanity.
They are but trifles, to be sure, scattered along life's pathway.
The good they do is inconceivable.
—Joseph Addison

When your children hear the word *mother,* what picture do they get in their mind's eye? Do they imagine a pleasant, encouraging woman with a warm expression and a cheerful disposition? A haggard lady shaking her head from side to side with a disappointed expression on her face? Or maybe an angry woman giving "the look"—you know, that fearful, pointed glare that could stop a raging bull in its tracks?

It's a little scary to speculate on what our children envision when they think of a "mother." We know the portrait we wish they'd have—the one we hope we give them more often than not! But how do we model the "warm and cheerful mom" when we feel more like the "haggard mom" after juggling an unending list of daily chores and responsibilities—or worse, like the "angry mom" after spending the day cleaning up spills, correcting bad attitudes, and disciplining wayward rugrats?

There are days when it can seem too difficult to even lift a smile when our kids come in the door after school or play. But a smile, physically speaking, is not a great burden. After all, it takes fewer facial muscles to create a smile than to produce a frown. And a simple smile, offered on a regular basis, can make a world of difference in the way our children view their days, their lives—and their mothers!

I know, it's hard to smile when we don't feel like it. But as positive moms, we need to recognize that a smile is less the result of a good feeling and more a gift that we give to others. When we give the simple gift of a smile, we lift the spirits of the people around us. We help them get through their day. Doesn't it work that way when someone smiles at you, whether you're at the shopping mall or at church or in your own home? Don't you feel uplifted, encouraged, as if someone likes you and believes in you? Don't you want to do the same for others—especially your kids?

A smile speaks volumes to our children. When a mother smiles at her son from the audience of a school play, she tells him, "I'm proud of you. You're doing a great job." When she smiles as her daughter comes in the door after a difficult day at school, she reassures her, "It's okay. Everything will be all right." When she grins from ear to ear as she picks up her ten-year-old from a week at summer camp, she says, "I missed you so much. I'm glad to see you! You are special to me."

I remember the impact my own mother's smile made on me when I competed on the school gymnastics team as a young girl. Even though I practiced and practiced, I continued to struggle with one particular move on the balance beam: the forward head roll. I seemed to lose my balance and fall off the beam every time!

I still had not mastered that roll by the time the first competition rolled around, so my sweet mother prayed with me before the meet, asking God to help me stay on the beam. Then she went into the stands to watch. Miraculously, when it was my turn to compete, I did the forward head roll without a slip! But as much as that accomplishment is etched in my memory, the moment I will never forget is when I looked up in the stands and saw my mother smiling. Her beaming face told me loud and clear: "I knew you could do it! Praise the Lord!"

Learn to greet your friends with a smile; they carry too many frowns in their own hearts to be bothered with yours. —Mary Allette Ayer

Don't Wait for the Feeling

Every moment of every day we have a choice as to what we will put on our face: a smile or a frown. We don't have to wait to have "happy feelings" before we smile. Think about it. Most of the actions we take in life are not based on a feeling but on a deliberate decision. You don't wait for the feeling to hit you before you do the laundry, do you? I hope not—otherwise you'd have piles of dirty clothes lying around just waiting for you to get a warm, fuzzy feeling about doing the wash. For most of us, I think, those piles would simply keep growing! No, you do the loads because they need to be done. It's not a matter of feeling like it; it's a matter of choosing a course of action. Smiling, too, is something we can choose to do whether we feel like it or not. It's an act of kindness—sometimes a sacrificial one—extended to those around us.

In his book *How to Win Friends and Influence People*, Dale Carnegie tells the story of a man in one of his classes who had a life-changing experience because of the power of a smile. The class had been instructed to smile at everyone they met for an entire week and then report back on the results. Here's Bill's story:

> When you asked me to make a talk about my experience with smiles, I thought I would try it for a week. So the next morning, while combing my hair, I looked at my glum mug in the mirror and said to myself: "Bill, you are going to wipe the scowl off that sour face of yours today. You are going to smile, and you are going to begin right now." As I sat down to breakfast, I greeted my wife with a "good morning, my dear!" And I smiled as I said it.
>
> You warned me that she might be surprised. Well, you underestimated her reaction. She was bewildered. She was shocked. I told her that in the future she could expect this as a regular occurrence, and I kept it up every morning. This changed attitude of mine has

brought more happiness into our home in the two months since I started than there was during the entire last year.

As I leave for my office, I greet the elevator operator in the apartment house with a "good morning," and I smile. I greet the doorman with a smile. I smile at the cashier in the subway booth when I ask for change. As I stand on the floor of the Stock Exchange, I smile at the people who until recently never saw me smile. I soon found that everybody was smiling back at me…

I am a totally different man; a happier man, a richer man, richer in friendships and happiness.[1]

Wow—the power of a smile! Notice Bill didn't wait for a feeling to hit him before he started sharing smiles with others. He just began smiling, and the feelings followed. Make the decision today to be a smiling mom and see what happens. You may want to forewarn your husband of your new objective; we don't want to cause any heart attacks!

The Basis for Smiling

Perhaps you are still not convinced that you can produce a smile when you don't feel like it. Consider what the Bible says about the characteristic of joy. Paul (I call him the "positive apostle") wrote to the early Christians about joy quite often. "Be joyful always," he wrote in 1 Thessalonians 5:16. "Rejoice in the Lord always," he said in Philippians 4:4. Now, this is a pretty amazing command when you consider that the early Christians faced persecution and even death for their faith in Christ! Many had friends and family members who'd already made that ultimate sacrifice—and for all they knew they could be next.

How could Paul expect them to rejoice in such circumstances? For this reason: True, biblical joy is not based on circumstances or feelings, but on something more substantial deep within our hearts.

There is a distinct difference between happiness and joy.

Happiness tends to be based on what happens in our lives. Suppose you get a knock at the door and a florist hands you a box filled with a dozen roses. A note from your spouse is attached, saying, "I'm proud of all you do. Keep up the great work!" No doubt a smile will erupt across your face due to the happiness you feel in that circumstance. Joy is different; it is there whether you get the roses or don't get the roses. It is a consistent attitude of peace, confidence, and satisfaction that resides deep within you because you know a loving God is a work in your life.

The early Christians didn't live in happy circumstances, yet Paul told them to "rejoice always." They could do that because they knew that Jesus Christ paid the penalty for their sins. They knew they were forgiven; they were deeply loved; and they had the assurance of eternal life. That deep sense of joy gave those early Christians a great and abiding strength that enabled them to face their difficult circumstances. The Old Testament hero Nehemiah explained this when he said, "The joy of the LORD is your strength" (Nehemiah 8:10).

Perhaps this kind of joy seems impossible to you. In a sense, it is. In the list of qualities that God produces in our lives through the Holy Spirit (known as the "fruit of the spirit" in Galatians 5:22–23), joy is the second quality named. We are not the producers of joy; God is! He develops joy in us as we get to know him, love him, and trust and obey his Word.

When we have true, godly joy, we experience a fulfilling gladness, deep satisfaction, and great pleasure. We have day-to-day confidence that "in all things God works for the good of those who love him, who have been called according to his purpose" (Romans 8:28). We can rejoice because we know that God is faithful and can be trusted to work through the good and the bad situations in our lives.

The word *joy* or *joyfulness* is mentioned more than 180 times in the

A cheerful heart is good medicine. —Proverbs 17:22

Old and New Testaments. If you still need help rejoicing, take some time to look them up using a Bible concordance. You can consider these two scriptures for a start:

> I delight greatly in the LORD;
>> my soul rejoices in my God.
> For he has clothed me with garments of salvation
>> and arrayed me in a robe of righteousness,
> as a bridegroom adorns his head like a priest
>> and as a bride adorns herself with her jewels.
>
> —Isaiah 61:10

> Then will I go to the altar of God,
>> to God, my joy and my delight.
> I will praise you with the harp,
>> O God, my God.
> Why are you downcast, O my soul?
>> Why so disturbed within me?
> Put your hope in God,
>> for I will yet praise him,
>> my Savior and my God.
>
> —Psalm 43:4–5

Like the early Christians, our reason to rejoice is our hope in God's salvation. Our wonderful and loving heavenly Father has provided forgiveness of our sins through his son, Jesus. He has given us the hope of eternal life as we put our faith in him. With Isaiah we can rejoice because he has clothed us in the "garments of salvation." With David, we can dispel worry, disappointment, and discouragement by putting our hope in God and choosing to say, "I will yet praise him, my Savior and my God." With Nehemiah, we can affirm that the joy of the Lord is all the strength we need to get through each day with a smile on our face.

Let Your Light Shine

Do you know people who seem to shine? Invariably, these are people who experience joy deep within their hearts. In fact, several references to joy in the Old Testament can be translated "to shine" (Psalm 21:1; Isaiah 9:3; Proverbs 23:24).

A joyful smile helps us to shine. It brightens the day for us and for everyone around us! And a little can go a long way. Think of the way one small, glowing candle can illuminate an entire dark room—that's how our smile can spread "Son-shine" into someone else's dark day. What greater gift can we give our kids than the example of a mom who shines for Christ?

Mother Teresa, the Nobel prize-winning nun who spent her life helping the sick and needy in Calcutta, India, always gave the gift of a smile to the hurting people she met. Listen to some of her thoughts about smiles:

> Peace begins with a smile—smile five times a day at someone you don't really want to smile at at all—do it for peace.

> Smile at one another. It is not always easy. Sometimes I find it hard to smile at my Sister, but then we must pray.[2]

If Mother Teresa could smile in the midst of the suffering and poverty that surrounded her, surely we can offer a smile from the warmth of our kitchens, surrounded by our precious loved ones!

Recently I asked my husband what he would like to have me do for him as he comes home from work each day. Did he want dinner on the table just as he walked in? Did he want a clean house upon his arrival (and if so, which room?) Would he like to hear some of his favorite music playing in the background?

Curt admitted that all the offers sounded good. But then he declined them, saying, "Karol, what I really need to see when I come home from work is a smile on your face. It makes my day when you greet me with a smile."

At first I was relieved that he had not picked one of the more difficult offers. But then I began to think of the downside. After all, I had worked hard to develop that just-right "haggard look" that would make Curt realize how difficult my day had been and cause him to feel sympathy for me as soon as he came in the door! As I thought about it, though, I had to admit "the look" hadn't been working as well as I'd hoped. And a smile, I figured, was an easy gift to give—much easier than dinner on the table on time.

Amazingly, as I made the effort in the days that followed, I found that I could produce a smile for Curt even on days when I wasn't feeling tremendously happy. I could even smile on PMS days! For about a year now I've kept the smiles coming, and you know what? My efforts have been infectious. These days we seem to have a contest to see who can greet Curt at the door first each evening—me, my girls, or the dogs. (I have to admit those faithful pooches beat me most of the time.) Curt enjoys his arrival at home each evening—and so do the rest of us.

I've found that my children also benefit from a smile when they come home after a long day of school or play. I make it a point to greet them with gladness when they emerge from the school building or hop in the car or walk in the door. The blessing I receive in return is to see them smile back!

A cheerful look sends an uplifting message that says, "Whether I feel it or not, there is something to smile about. There is something in our lives for which we can be glad!" Our children and family members need to hear that message—and so do we.

A Time and Place for Everything

Of course, there is a time and a place for everything. A smile is appropriate much of the time—but there *are* times when it is out of

Rejoice in the Lord always. I will say it again: Rejoice! —Philippians 4:4

place. I'm not suggesting that we smile 100 percent of every day for the rest of our lives. Solomon put it best when he said, "There is a time for everything, and a season for every activity under heaven…a time to weep and a time to laugh, a time to mourn and a time to dance" (Ecclesiastes 3:1, 4).

A positive mom, generally speaking, is a smiling mom. Our kids will become smiling kids as they learn from our example. But we need to be *real* moms as well. When the circumstances of life call for a cry, we must weep out of the depths of our being. When there is reason to mourn, we must mourn thoroughly and completely. Expressing sadness or loss doesn't mean that God's joy has left us; it simply means that we are not afraid to show our emotions and be transparent about our feelings. Joy is deeper, remember? A quiet, joyful peace can still reside within us even as we work through sadness, grief, and pain.

When I was thirty years old, a car tragically killed my mother while she was crossing a street during her routine morning walk. This was a devastating time for me and my family. Everyone loved Grammy. We cried and grieved together—but were never without the peace of knowing that God was at work in our lives. We had the assurance that my mother, a godly woman, was in heaven with the Lord. Did we smile? No, this was not the time for smiling; it was the time for grieving. But when our grieving had run its course, the smiles returned.

The True Worth of a Smile

Several years ago our family took a trip to Florida. In the small but quaint town of Appalachicola, I found a unique item in a little gift shop. It was called "Smile on a Stick" and was actually a cardboard picture of a smile mounted on a craft stick. For the bargain price of $1.75, you could hold it in front of your mouth anytime you wanted to smile!

If you see this little gadget in your own travels, let me encourage you: Don't buy it! You already have a smile. It costs you nothing, but it's worth a million bucks. Start giving your smile away as a gift to the people around you, whether you feel like it or not; you'll find that the feelings will follow, and you will be the richer for it.

Smiles are contagious. Let's infect our family members—and everyone else we meet—with ours. Think how much brighter our lives will be with all those shining faces around us!

After all, with the joy we find only in Christ, we have reason to smile.

POWER POINT

Read: John 3:29; 15:11; 16:20–24; and 17:13. Underline the word *joy* every time you see it. Notice the basis for joy in each of these verses.

Pray: Dear wonderful and loving heavenly Father, I praise you for the salvation I have in you. Thank you that through Jesus my sins are forgiven and I have the hope of eternal life. Thank you that your joy can be my strength through the ups and downs of life. Thank you for the ability to smile. Help me to give this gift of a smile to my family and friends. Help my children to learn to experience joy in life as they watch my example. In Jesus' name, amen.

Do: Choose a day this week to give everyone you come in contact with the gift of a sincere smile. Share with your husband, your children, or a friend how your experience with smiles touched you and touched others.

Principle #2

THe
Pwer
OF
Prayer

The prayer of a righteous man is powerful and effective.
—James 5:16

*Prayer is a sincere, sensible, affectionate pouring out of the soul
to God, through Christ, in the strength and assistance of the Spirit,
for such things as God has promised.*
—John Bunyan

A Positive Mom Is a Praying Mom
How to Effectively Pray for Your Kids

I know not by what methods rare,
But this I know; God answers prayer.
I know not if the blessing sought Will come in just the guise I thought.
I leave my prayer to Him alone Whose will is wiser than my own.
—Eliza M. Hickok

The famous preacher Billy Sunday told the story of a young minister who enjoyed visiting the families in his church during the week. At one home, a child answered the door and politely invited him in. When the minister asked to see her mother, the young girl replied, "You cannot see mother, for she prays from nine to ten." The minister decided to wait.

After forty minutes the woman finally emerged from her "prayer closet." Her face was filled with such a bright glow that the minister knew immediately why this woman's home was such a haven of peace and order, and why her oldest daughter was a missionary and her two sons were in the ministry. Billy Sunday finished the story by saying, "All hell cannot tear a boy or girl away from a praying mother."[1]

Do you want to make a positive impact on the next generation? Become a praying mom! Many men, women, boys, and girls have been kept from falling into sin, foolishness, and destruction because their mothers' knees were bent in prayer. Jesus said, "Ask and it will be given to you; seek and you will find; knock and the door will be opened to you. For everyone who asks receives; he who seeks finds; and to him who knocks, the door will be opened" (Matthew 7:7–8). Are you willing to take God at his word and ask him to help and bless your family?

Why Pray?

Jesus also said, "Your Father knows what you need before you ask him" (Matthew 6:8). If God already knows all of our needs, is it really necessary to tell him in prayer? Perhaps your children have asked you this question—and if they haven't yet, they will. You need the answer for their sake as well as yours. Why do we pray if God knows everything?

1. We Pray Because God Tells Us to Bring All Our Requests to Him

Jesus' statement about God knowing our needs before we verbalize them was not intended to discourage prayer—just to discourage long and showy prayers. We don't need to impress God (or the people around us) with our ability to spout windy, pious-sounding prayers! Prayer, Jesus said, is actually best when kept personal and simple. He followed that statement by teaching his disciples the simple model for prayer we know today as "The Lord's Prayer" (Matthew 6:9–13).

Later, in the Garden of Gethsemane, he instructed his followers to "watch and pray" (Matthew 26:41). He himself prayed—in the garden and throughout his life and ministry. His followers also called people to pray. "You do not have, because you do not ask God," James reminds us (James 4:2). "Do not be anxious about anything, but in everything, by prayer and petition, with thanksgiving, present your requests to God," Paul says in Philippians 4:6.

2. We Pray Because We Need Wisdom from Above to Be Good Mothers

Frankly, we need wisdom to survive this job of motherhood—and the source of all true wisdom is God. "For the LORD gives wisdom, and from his mouth come knowledge and understanding" (Proverbs 2:6). There is no parenting book we can read or family seminar we can attend that will give us the answer to every problem that arises in our children's lives. We need God's help! Fortunately, he promises to give us wisdom if we ask for it: "If any of you lacks wisdom, he should ask God, who gives generously to all without finding fault, and it will be given to him" (James 1:5).

Isn't it inspiring to think that the creator of the universe is willing to give us wisdom if we just ask? But wisdom is not the only thing we need as mothers. We should also pray for patience, strength, peace, perseverance—and the list could go on and on. When we pray, we can be confident that God will give us everything we need. Jesus said in Mark 11:24, "Therefore I tell you, whatever you ask for in prayer, believe that you have received it, and it will be yours."

I remember a particularly challenging time in my life as a young mother when prayer became a solace and a necessity to me. Grace was two years old and Joy was six months old, and I felt out of my league. I had neither the patience to handle a child in the "trying twos" nor the strength to meet the needs of a demanding baby. Day after day I found myself both frazzled and frustrated, often displaying my emotions in tears in front of Curt and the kids. And as if that weren't overwhelming enough, we were in the process of moving our little family into a new house—no small feat under the best of circumstances.

My prayer life, I must admit, had dwindled to little more than a few whispered words as I cleaned up the dinner dishes. After all, who has time to pray when you have a bottle to warm, diapers to change, a toddler to chase, loads of laundry to fold, and boxes to pack and unpack?

Have you ever felt overwhelmed by the circumstances of life? Perhaps my situation seems like a piece of cake compared to what you've gone through. Or maybe you, too, have experienced a number of small frustrations adding up and eating away at your joy and strength. Whatever our situations, we all have times when we feel unable to handle or control our circumstances. Those are the times when we need prayer the most.

During those trying months I began to recognize my true need for help from above. Clearly I didn't have the power within myself to renew my physical or emotional strength. Only God could do that. So I began to pray that God would help me organize my tasks and give me the strength and direction I needed. I even asked him to help me make more time for prayer. And as I gave my cares and anxieties over to him, I began to experience a wonderful new peace and calm in my heart and in my home. The scripture in Isaiah 40:28–31 came alive to me:

> Do you not know? Have you not heard? The LORD is the everlasting God, the Creator of the ends of the earth. He will not grow tired or weary, and his understanding no one can fathom. He gives strength to the weary and increases the power of the weak. Even youths grow tired and weary, and young men stumble and fall; but those who hope in the LORD will renew their strength. They will soar on wings like eagles; they will run and not grow weary, they will walk and not be faint.

3. We Pray Because Our Families Need Our Fervent Prayers

No matter how good we are as mothers, we can't be our children's sole protector and provider. We can't be their around-the-clock bodyguard. No, only God can be in all places at all times; only he has the power to watch over every family member every moment as we scatter in the morning to work, school, or play. We must entrust our precious ones to God daily in prayer, recognizing our dependence on him for their physical and spiritual health and safety.

The Old Testament character Hannah is a wonderful example of a praying mom—a mother who diligently, faithfully, and persistently sought the Lord for her needs and the needs of her family. Unable to have children of her own, she nevertheless prayed earnestly that God would give her a son. She deeply, desperately wanted a child. If God would give her a son, she promised, she would "give him to the LORD for all the days of his life" (1 Samuel 1:11). God heard the prayer of this devoted woman, and eventually a son—Samuel—was born.

True to her promise, Hannah took young Samuel to live with Eli the priest. You would think that a priest's home would be a safe and nurturing place to grow up. But while Eli himself was a good man, his two sons were evil. Imagine Hannah leaving her precious son—her very own answer to prayer—in a household with two wicked brothers! No doubt Hannah continued her petitions to God, praying for her son's protection. As a result, Samuel "continued to grow in stature and in favor with the LORD and with men" (1 Samuel 2:26). Eventually he became God's prophet, a true man of God who led the nation of Israel for many years.

We can sum up Hannah's story—and our own responsibility to pray for our families—with a paraphrase of James 5:16: "The effective, fervent prayer of a righteous mom avails much" (NKJV). Our families need our fervent prayers if they are to become everything God intends for them to be. Their physical health and spiritual growth will not go unnoticed and unchallenged. The Bible tells us, "Your enemy the devil prowls around like a roaring lion looking for someone to devour" (1 Peter 5:8). He would love to sink his teeth into our children and cut them off from the future God has planned for them. For their sakes we must "resist him" (v. 9)—and we can do that best on our knees.

Hannah could not be with Samuel as he grew up. But, fortunately, she was a woman of prayer, and we can gain inspiration and encouragement from her example. Like Hannah, we will not be able to hold our

Be joyful always; pray continually. —1 Thessalonians 5:16–17

children's hands every time they face a challenge or hit a bump in the road. But we can pray for them and rest assured that God is with them, watching over them and molding them into the people he wants them to be.

Pray without Ceasing

One of my favorite verses as a child was 1 Thessalonians 5:17: "Never stop praying" (PHILLIPS). I loved this verse because it was short and easy for a ten-year-old to memorize (which meant an easy sticker in Sunday school!) As an adult, and especially as a mother, I still love this verse. Now more than ever I recognize that continual prayer is more than a nice idea; it's an absolute necessity—a moment-by-moment recognition of my dependence on God to meet the numerous responsibilities, decisions, and concerns that arise each day.

But can a person really pray continually, without stopping? Bible scholars say this command can be understood two ways. One interpretation is that we must continually be in an *attitude* of prayer hour by hour and day by day, constantly talking to the Father as we go about our daily work and routine. Mother Teresa was a wonderful model of this attitude of prayer. She once said there was only one reason she was able to minister faithfully day in and day out to the poorest of the poor in Calcutta: "I pray!" She went on to explain, "You should spend at least half an hour in the morning and an hour at night in prayer. You can pray while you work. Work doesn't stop prayer, and prayer doesn't stop work. It requires only that small raising of mind to Him. 'I love You, God, I trust You, I believe in You, I need You now.' Small things like that. They are wonderful prayers."[2]

Perhaps you have found, as I have, that there are many opportunities to turn our thoughts heavenward during a typical day. We can pray as we fold the laundry, lifting up prayers for the recipient of each freshly cleaned item. As we set the table, we can pray for the one who will be seated at each place. We can pray as we cook dinner or wash dishes. We can pray as we drive our children to different practices and events, and we can certainly pray as they perform or participate in those activities. We should pray as we drop them off at school or day care or a friend's home. Never stop praying! A positive mom is a praying mom.

A second interpretation of the command to "pray without ceasing" is that we must never allow our prayer life to fall by the wayside. It is important that we set aside a regular time for prayer and stay devoted to it, never letting it get choked out by the busyness of motherhood and the distractions of our daily routines. We need a time each day to purposefully, lovingly, and deliberately pray—a set time when we praise God for who he is, thank him for what he has done and is doing in our lives, and lay before him our cares, worries, and requests (more on this in the next chapter). "Sometimes we think we are too busy to pray," C. H. Spurgeon once said. "That is a great mistake, for praying is a saving of time."

Jesus, of course, is the best example of someone who never allowed anything to keep him from being a person of prayer. Scripture is full of scenes of Jesus praying to the Father. And if the *Son of God* felt compelled to pray, shouldn't we pray as well?

We read in Mark 1:35, "Very early in the morning, while it was still dark, Jesus got up, left the house and went off to a solitary place, where he prayed." Notice, the scripture says Jesus got up "while it was still dark." Sorry, all you non-morning people, but early in the day does seem to be a particularly good time to lift our cares heavenward! Listen to the words of the psalmist: "In the morning, O LORD, you hear my voice; in the morning I lay my requests before you and wait in expectation" (Psalm 5:3).

Personally, I like to get up early each morning, before anyone else is

This is the confidence we have in approaching God: that if we ask anything according to his will, he hears us. And if we ask—we know that we have what we asked of him. —1 John 5:14-15

stirring, and sit down at my kitchen table for a time of prayer and study. There, with a cup of coffee and an open Bible, I meet with God. I relish the quiet stillness of the household at that hour and the wonderful embrace of my heavenly Father in the alone time. As I read the Scriptures each morning, recognizing that they are God's love letters to me, I grow to love him more and more. In prayer, I pour out my requests to him and lay my anxieties at his feet. I praise him for who he is and what he means to my life. Occasionally one of my girls will come into the kitchen and find me with my head bowed over God's Word, but that's okay. I believe my children need to see that prayer is important to me and that I depend on God for each day's strength.

I'm not suggesting that you *must* be an early riser to have a fulfilling prayer life, but first-thing-in-the-morning prayer does have some definite advantages. For mothers especially, the most peaceful time of the day tends to be in the morning, before the other members of the household are up and running. Why not start getting up just a few minutes earlier each day to pray? You will soon find that you enjoy getting up early and beginning your mornings alone with God.

Notice that Mark 1:35 also says that Jesus went to a "solitary place" to pray. If it were only that easy! Finding a solitary place often presents a unique challenge for mothers. Generally speaking, wherever we go—anywhere in the house—*they* will find us. Funny how we can even retreat to the privacy (we think) of the bathroom and not have two minutes of quiet before we hear a knock on the door and see little fingers poking underneath. Yes, it is hard for moms to get away!

The opportunity to find a little solitude is another good reason for praying early in the morning. But sometimes, no matter how early we try to rise, some little tyke will beat us to the breakfast table. If that's what regularly happens to you, don't despair! Instead, choose a small room or large closet in your house and designate it as your special "prayer place." Then instruct the rest of the family to respect your time when you're in that place. You may even want to hang a sign on the door that reads:

```
MIP
Mother in Prayer
Please Do Not Disturb
```

If you have a young baby and feel you cannot physically "get away" for a few minutes, try simply holding your little bundle in your arms while you pray. After all, our children are only that young and cuddly for a short time; go ahead and relish the opportunity to hold and cuddle your baby while you pray! The purpose for finding a solitary place is to minimize the distractions of the household and help us stay focused on our conversation with God. If you can pray with your baby in your arms, go for it.

Think of your prayer time this way: If you were planning to get together with your best friend to chat about the important issues in your lives, would you choose to meet in a room with lots of noise, activity, and constant interruptions? I didn't think so! We need to plan our conversations with God with similar thoughtfulness and care.

Praying with Confidence

Howard Chandler Robbins once said, "The prayers of the Christian are secret, but their effect cannot be hidden."[3] Certainly that was true in the life of Englishman George Muller, considered to be one of the mightiest men of prayer of the nineteenth century. While founding a number of successful orphanages for the children of England, Muller determined to never ask anyone for money to meet his needs or the needs of the orphans. Instead he committed all of those needs to prayer. Amazingly he raised more than eight million dollars (think how much that would be in today's money!) by directing his petitions not to men, but to God. Somehow God always made sure Muller received all the resources he needed.

Muller never prayed for things just because he wanted them, or even because he felt they were needed for God's work. No, before praying, he would search the Scriptures to find if there was a promise in God's Word that covered the circumstance or need in question. Sometimes he would search the Bible for days before presenting his petition to God. What devotion!

When he found the appropriate promise, Muller would then place his finger on that spot in his open Bible and plead with God based on the assurance of God's own Word. As mothers, we can devote ourselves to prayer in the same way. Perhaps you can set aside a Bible in the household for use as your family's "prayer Bible." Highlight the passages and promises you want to pray for you and your family. (You may want to use a different color marker for each family member.)

Here are some passages that contain promises you will certainly want to highlight:

- *Comfort and peace:* Psalm 42; 2 Corinthians 1:3–5; 4:7–12; Philippians 4:6–7

- *Family relationships:* Deuteronomy 6:4–9; Proverbs 22:6; Ephesians 5:21–6:4

- *Faith and character:* Matthew 6:25–34; Galatians 5:16–26; Colossians 1:9–12; 3:13–15

- *Love for others:* Mark 12:30–35; 1 John 4:7–10; Hebrews 10:24; 1 Corinthians 13

- *God's provision:* Matthew 6:25–34; 7:11

- *Strength:* Psalms 9:9; 34:4; 37:23; 69:22; 73:26; 138:7; Ephesians 6:10–18; 2 Timothy 4:16–17

- *Wisdom:* Proverbs 2:6; James 1:5

- *Faith:* Hebrews 11

- *Joy:* Nehemiah 8:10; Isaiah 12; Galatians 5:22

- *Safety:* Psalms 46; 91

Like George Muller, we can pray with confidence when we know our prayers are based on God's unchanging Word. Thomas Watson put it this way: "God's promises are the cork to keep faith from sinking in prayer."[4]

Praying Specifically for Your Children

Prayer is the most powerful force available to us in raising our children. It is not enough that we give our kids food, clothing, shelter, education, or any other benefit. To be positive, godly moms, we need to pray for them—continually. In addition to the general scriptures listed above, there are many Bible verses that deal specifically with the needs of our children and the direction they need to go in order to live godly lives. Here are some prayers and related scriptures to help you get started:

- Pray that they will come to know Christ and follow him (Romans 10:9–11).

- Pray that they will be able to recognize evil and hate it (Psalm 97:10).

- Pray that when they do something wrong, they are caught (Psalm 119:71).

- Pray for their protection against the evil one (John 17:15).

- Pray that they would be kind and forgiving toward others (Ephesians 4:32).

- Pray that they'll have courage to stand up for what is right (Joshua 1:7).

- Pray that they will have respect for authority (Romans 13:1).

- Pray that they choose wise friends (Proverbs 13:20).

- Pray for their future spouse, that they will marry a godly person (2 Corinthians 6:14–17).

- Pray for them to submit to God and resist the devil (James 4:7).

- Pray for a hedge of protection around them (Hosea 2:6).

Don't stop with these verses; search the Scriptures for yourself and find all the wonderful truths and promises you can pray for on behalf of your family. I promise this effort will revolutionize your prayer life. I know it did mine. Not long ago I went to a book resale shop and bought a Bible to use specifically for my prayer time. I don't hesitate to mark it up, and I attach different colors of "sticky notes" to identify scripture promises I want to pray for each of my family members. I pray with confidence for my husband, children, and other loved ones as I point (like George Muller) to God's promises in his Word!

In addition to your prayer Bible, I recommend that you begin to record your prayers—along with the answers you receive—in a notebook or journal. Many moms (and others) have found that the simple act of writing down prayer requests each day provides a tangible reminder that those requests have been turned over to God. We know that we have cast those cares on him. We don't have to worry about them anymore!

And as we record the answers to prayer that God gives us, we find that our faith is strengthened and our desire to pray is increased. We begin approaching our heavenly Father with a greater sense of awe and gratitude. You know, sometimes we need to be reminded to thank the Lord for responding to our prayers! How sad it would be if we were like the nine lepers in Luke 17:11–19 who never returned to thank Jesus after he healed them of their terrible disease. As positive moms, we need to be like the tenth leper who ran to Jesus and fell at his feet, full of gratitude and praise to God.

In the years to come, when you look back over your prayer journal, you will feel as if you're taking a stroll down Memory Lane and a walk through Thanksgiving Park. You will be blessed to see how far God has brought you and what he has done in your life—and in the lives of each family member for whom you have prayed.

Never Give Up

As positive, praying moms, we need to be persistent in our prayers and never give up. Jesus made this point in a parable about a persistent widow in Luke 18:1–8. In this story, the widow went repeatedly to a judge to seek justice for a wrong that had been done to her. But the judge neither feared God nor cared about the people in his jurisdiction, and he sent her away each time. The widow was persistent, however, and she continued to cry out to the judge. Finally he said to himself, "Even though I don't fear God or care about men, yet because this widow keeps bothering me, I will see that she gets justice, so that she won't eventually wear me out with her coming!" (vv. 4–5).

Jesus capped off the parable by saying, "Listen to what the unjust judge says. And will not God bring about justice for his chosen ones, who cry out to him day and night? Will he keep putting them off? I tell you, he will see that they get justice, and quickly" (vv. 6–8).

If the inconsiderate judge finally gave in to the widow's pleas, how much more will our loving heavenly Father hear our persistent requests and respond with kindness toward us? Never stop praying! The saying is true: We are never so high as when we are on our knees in prayer. Begin to reach to new and greater heights. Be a praying mom!

POWER POINT

Read: The story of Hannah in 1 Samuel 1 and her prayer of thanksgiving in 1 Samuel 2:1–10.

Pray: I praise you, most loving and kind Father, for hearing my prayers. It is incredible to think that the God of the universe would want to have a conversation with me! Thank you for allowing me to come to you with my needs and requests. Thank you for loving my family more perfectly and more deeply than I could ever love them. You are truly "our refuge and strength, an ever-present help in trouble" (Psalm 46:1). Help me to be a woman of prayer and a diligent and faithful prayer warrior for my family. In Jesus' name, amen.

Do: Decide on a time that would be best for you to spend in prayer each day, then choose a private place where you can be alone during that interval. Write the time and place in your calendar or day planner. Place a Bible, pen, and prayer journal in your place of prayer so it can be waiting there for you each day.

Casting Your Cares
Finding Strength, Hope, and Wisdom for Each Day

Every evening I turn my worries over to God.
He's going to be up all night anyway.
—Mary C. Crowley

About once a year at our house, we overhaul the junk closet. We rummage through the layers of old shoes, broken toys, worn-out backpacks, and other sundry items, and throw out everything that has been outgrown or gone unused. I'm not quite sure how all the stuff accumulates there each year, but it sure feels good to dig in and finally get rid of the excess baggage.

Whether it's a junk closet, a catchall drawer, or an overloaded purse, most of us have a place where we store things that we probably should have thrown out or given away long before. We feel so good when we finally get serious and unload the clutter that we wonder why we didn't do it sooner!

As mothers, we have a tendency to hold on to things we shouldn't—and I'm not just talking about old bowling balls, broken umbrellas, and worn-out tennis shoes. Too often we allow the cares of life to pile up in the closet in our hearts called "worry." Just as we clean out the junk in our home closets on a regular basis, we need to continually cast off the worries that we collect and tuck away in our hearts. And while we might reasonably clean out a junk closet once or twice a year, we should tackle our worries on a daily basis.

Perhaps you are thinking, "What's the big deal? Doesn't everyone worry? What's so bad about savoring some anxieties and enjoying a little apprehension now and then? I'm a mother. I've earned it!"

Well, what does God want us to do with worry: relish it or relinquish it? The apostle Paul is quite clear on this subject. "Do not be anxious about anything, but in everything, by prayer and petition, with thanksgiving, present your requests to God," he writes in Philippians 4:6–7. "And the peace of God, which transcends all understanding, will guard your hearts and your minds in Christ Jesus." Notice, Paul doesn't say, *"Consider* getting rid of anxiety." No, he is quite straightforward: "Do not be anxious."

In the Sermon on the Mount, Jesus also addressed the topic of worry:

> Therefore I tell you, do not worry about your life, what you will eat or drink; or about your body, what you will wear. Is not life more important than food, and the body more important than clothes? Look at the birds of the air; they do not sow or reap or store away in barns, and yet your heavenly Father feeds them. Are you not much more valuable than they? Who of you by worrying can add a single hour to his life?
>
> And why do you worry about clothes? See how the lilies of the field grow. They do not labor or spin. Yet I tell you that not even Solomon in all his splendor was dressed like one of these. If that is how God clothes the grass of the field which is here today and tomorrow is thrown into the fire, will he not much more clothe you, O you of little faith? So do not worry, saying, "What shall we eat?" or "What shall we drink?" or "What shall we wear?" For the pagans run after all these things, and your heavenly Father knows that you need them. But seek first his kingdom and his righteousness, and all these things will be given to you as well. Therefore do not worry about tomorrow, for tomorrow will worry about itself. Each day has enough trouble of its own. (Matthew 6:25–34)

Once again we are told in no uncertain terms that we are not supposed to worry. The truth is, when we wallow in worry and give in to our anxious fears, we are actually disobeying the instructions of the Bible! Have you ever thought of worry as disobedience? In our culture, fear, anxiety, and worry have become so commonplace that few people realize that they are disobeying God when they do these things.

Author and motivational speaker Ed Foreman describes worry as "nothing less than the misuse of your imagination."[1] What do you tend to worry about? What makes your mind run off and begin to imagine everything bad that could possibly happen? The list of worry prompters is different for each of us, but we all have areas that we find difficult to release fully to God. Some of us worry about finances; others, our children's safety; others, what people think about us. Some of us worry about all three—and then keep going. Sometimes we can feel as if we're drowning in the imaginary oceans we create with our persistent worrying.

Why do we harbor and savor our worries like that? Could it be that worrying is easy, but faith is difficult?

Worry and faith are mutually exclusive! They're opposites. God doesn't want us to live in fear and anxiety because when we do, we are not practicing faith in his loving care and provision. What we're really saying is, "God, I don't think you will come through for me on this one, so I need to concern myself with this problem."

That's not faith; that's fear—and it's rampant in our society. It's even rampant in our churches! In fact, anxious fear is such a common human problem that the Bible often tells us not to be afraid. The command "be not afraid" appears more than twenty times in the Old Testament alone.

Choosing Faith, Not Fear

Consider the story of Jehoshaphat, one of the ancient kings of Judah, found in 2 Chronicles 20:1–30. This faithful king was under attack by a vast fighting force—the combined armies of three of Israel's worst enemies. Though alarmed by the situation, King Jehoshaphat chose not to pace the floor fretfully and wring his hands in worry. Instead he declared a time of fasting and prayer and sought help from God.

A prophet arrived and gave this word of hope to Jehoshaphat: "This is what the LORD says to you: 'Do not be afraid or discouraged because of this vast army. For the battle is not yours, but God's'" (v. 15). The king then turned to his people as they left for battle and said, "Listen to me, Judah and people of Jerusalem! Have faith in the LORD your God and you will be upheld" (v. 20). And they were! The Lord set ambushes against their enemies, and the three armies that had allied themselves against Israel ended up destroying one other.

Yes, the circumstances were challenging, but God was with the people of Judah as they looked to him for their strength. In fact, drawing strength from God to overcome fear and worry is a recurring theme in Bible history. Long before Jehoshaphat, for example, Joshua was chosen to be Moses' successor to lead the nation of Israel into the Promised Land. Now, how would you feel if you were handed the responsibility for leading millions of grumbling people with no military training through the wilderness and into a land inhabited by fierce armies? A tad bit anxious? But God did not allow Joshua to wallow in worry; instead, he gave him this message of hope: "Have I not commanded you? Be strong and courageous. Do not be terrified; do not be discouraged, for the LORD your God will be with you wherever you go" (Joshua 1:9).

Joshua, like Jehoshaphat, was a person of great faith. In fact, I believe the reason God chose Joshua to be the leader of Israel was because he had proven himself to be a man who lived out his faith in God. Remember when Moses sent Joshua, Caleb, and ten other Hebrews to spy out the Promised Land? Joshua and Caleb returned from their mission with confidence and hope, encouraging Moses to "go for it" because God would surely be with them. "We should go up and take possession of the land, for we can certainly do it," Caleb said (Numbers 13:30). But the other spies worried and fretted, telling Moses that the enemies in the land across the Jordan River were much too great for Israel to tackle. By their worry, the ten showed their lack of faith. They didn't believe God was big enough or dependable enough to help them defeat the opposition! As a result, those fretting spies never made it into the Promised Land.

You may not be leading an army into a foreign country, but you are leading a family into a future mapped out for them by God. To be a positive mom, faith is crucial. "And without faith it is impossible to please God," Hebrews 11:6 says. The way we choose faith—and resist the tendency to be worried and afraid—is to give our cares over to God each day in prayer.

Life with a View

The story is told of an old widow who lived with her two sons in San Francisco. They were immigrants from Asia and depended entirely on the boys' earnings to meet their living expenses. Fortunately, the sons were enterprising young men and had their own small businesses—one selling rain ponchos and the other selling sunglasses. Still, every day the mother wore herself out with fret and worry. If she looked out the window and saw that the day would be sunny, she became filled with anxiety, worrying that no one would purchase her first son's ponchos. If it looked like rain, she would become desperately afraid that no one would buy her second son's sunglasses. No matter how the weather turned out, it seemed this woman always had something to worry about!

With this anxious outlook on life, she was continually glum—until a kind neighbor told her she was looking at it all wrong.

"Instead of being anxious all of the time," the neighbor suggested, "you should be joyful each day. After all, no matter what the weather brings, at least one of your sons will have a successful day!"

From then on, the woman's outlook changed, and she lived out the rest of her years with an abiding sense of happiness and peace. You see, perspective is everything! Are we able to see all of life's circumstances in the hands of a loving Lord who wants the best for us, or do we worry and fret about how we can make things work out for ourselves?

Joseph, the son of Jacob in the Old Testament, had a good perspective on life. Although Joseph was well loved by his father, his eleven brothers hated him—so much so that they threw him in a pit and sold him as a slave. Joseph could have given up on life at that point, thinking God had left him. But Scripture is clear that he continued to have faith that God had a great plan for his life.

Joseph was sold to a man in Egypt named Potiphar and rose to a position of responsibility in that household. Things were definitely looking up—until a false accusation brought an end to Joseph's prosperity and landed him in prison. Amazingly there is nothing in Scripture to indicate that Joseph was worried, despite these new circumstances. Instead he kept looking to God, who showed himself faithful to Joseph over and over.

One day Joseph was brought out of prison and given the opportunity to interpret one of the Pharaoh's ominous dreams. Stepping out on faith, Joseph trusted God to tell him what the dream meant. When Joseph shared the interpretation that God gave him, the Pharoah was so impressed that he elevated the former prisoner to second-in-command in all of Egypt. God continued to bless Joseph with wisdom; and through Joseph's foresight, the Egyptians were able to avoid the ravages of a severe famine that hit the region several years later.

What was Joseph's perspective on life? Faith! We catch a glimpse of his faith in his response to his scoundrel brothers, who begged him for

Prayer puts God's work in his hands—and keeps it there. —E. M. Bounds mercy for their abuse so many years before. "Don't be afraid," Joseph said. "Am I in the place of God? You intended to harm me, but God intended it for good to accomplish what is now being done, the saving of many lives" (Genesis 50:19–20). Joseph acknowledged both the good and the bad in his life. But because of his perspective of faith, he understood that every challenge he encountered was God's way of working toward a bigger picture in his life.

How do you approach the challenges in your life? Do you see them as an opportunity to worry—or an opportunity to trust God?

I believe God works in our lives like a jigsaw puzzle. One piece looks nice; another is ugly. One piece fits in an obvious place; another seems to fit nowhere at all. Some pieces are unidentifiable in themselves; but as they are connected with the rest of the pieces and put in proper perspective, they begin to create a wonderful picture.

We face many different situations in life—some we understand and some we don't; some that are pleasant and others that are just plain awful. Our faith comes in as we trust God with the big picture, recognizing that he has a plan for our lives. We can stand confidently on the words of Romans 8:28: "And we know that in all things God works for the good of those who love him, who have been called according to his purpose."

Some friends of ours are a case in point. Several years ago, they went through a difficult time with their finances. After losing a job, they fell into debt and eventually lost their large, beautiful home. Of course, they never would have asked for such tragedy; but the result was that they became totally dependent on God as they prayed for a new job and for help to meet their daily needs. They talked openly about their struggles and their new journey of faith, encouraging many people in the process. Today they are back on their feet financially, but with new priorities and a new perspective on life. They truly believe that their time of crisis was ultimately a blessing for their family.

Living Day by Day

I find the job of washing dishes downright frustrating, don't you? After you wash all the dishes from a meal, low and behold, you eat another meal and have to wash them all over again! You can't say, "Well, I finished that load. Now I'll never need to wash another dish." It doesn't work that way!

Many or our responsibilities as mothers require that kind of continual, repetitive attention: the laundry, dusting, vacuuming, cooking, even changing diapers (up to a point). Casting our cares on the Lord should be a daily responsibility as well. Funny how old worries tend to sneak back into our hearts and minds, just like the dust that keeps reappearing on the furniture. But rather than be discouraged when a particular worry rears its head again, we can consider its reappearance as an opportunity to once again cast our cares where they belong: in God's hands.

When I was in high school, I made a "God Box." It was pretty simple really; I took a shoebox, wrapped it with construction paper, and put a slit in the top. Then whenever I found that I was worrying about a particular issue in my life, I wrote the concern on an index card and placed it in the God Box. This was a physical, visual way for me to recognize that I was giving that care over to the Lord. Whenever the anxious thought came back to my mind, I would remind myself that I had already placed that worry in God's hands.

Recently I spray-painted a similar shoebox for our family and cut a slit in the top. I'm convinced that with the trails and worries that tend to accompany and complicate the middle school years, my daughters (and I!) will really need a God Box.

It is amazing how much time and energy we can save if we do not spend our days worrying! We can even feel better physically if we make it a habit to cast our cares daily on God. As Dr. Charles Mayo explains, "Worry affects circulation, the heart and the glands, the whole nervous system, and profoundly affects the heart. I have never known a man who died from overwork, but many who died from doubt."[2]

Worry also has a stifling effect on our creativity and ability to live life to the full.

Consider the little clock that worked herself into a frenzy because she began thinking about how often she would have to tick in the coming year. She thought to herself, "I'll have to tick two times per second, which means 120 ticks per minute, 7,200 ticks per hour, and 172,800 ticks each day!" As she continued to calculate the challenges before her, she began to feel a sense of panic. She couldn't possibly complete 1,209,600 ticks every week, which meant nearly 63 million ticks in the coming year! The more she thought about the enormity of her task, the more she worried—until she finally felt so overwhelmed that her little ticker began to go on the blink.

Realizing her need for help, the dismayed clock visited a counselor. "I just don't have what it takes to tick so much in one year," she lamented.

"How many ticks must you tick at one time?" the wise counselor asked.

"Just one at a time," the clock responded.

The counselor smiled, saying, "If you use your energy to tick just one tick at a time, I think you will be just fine."

The little clock left that day with a new outlook, wound herself up, and began to concern herself with just one tick at a time. And as you can imagine, she ticked happily ever after.

Aren't you thankful we can't see into the future of our lives or the lives of our children? We might want to give up if we knew some of the challenges that await us! Instead, because we don't know what the future holds, we must trust God. I think of Corrie Ten Boom, who lovingly trusted her heavenly Father. If she would have known as a young girl that she and her family members would be sent to concentration

Cast all your anxiety on him because he cares for you. —1 Peter 5:7

☺

camps for harboring Jews during World War II, she might have shrunk back in fear from the destiny God had for her. But God gave her—as he gives us—the grace to handle life one day at a time.

Corrie tells the story of a particularly anxious time in her life. Her father sat down on the edge of her bed and said, "Corrie, when you and I go to Amsterdam—when do I give you your ticket?" She sniffed and said, "Why, just before we get on the train." Her father responded, "Exactly. And our wise Father in heaven knows when we're going to need things, too. Don't run out ahead of him, Corrie. When the time comes that some of us will have to die, you will look into your heart and find the strength you need—just in time."[3]

Corrie Ten Boom faced severe persecution in her life, but she experienced great faith, as well. Don't worry about tomorrow; today has enough cares of its own. Take your cares to the One who cares! He will be faithful to give you the grace you need when you need it.

To God Be the Glory

We give God glory—and draw others to him—when we learn to lay our anxieties daily at the feet of Jesus. As we cast our cares on him, God gives us a deep and profound peace that "transcends all understanding" (Philippians 4:7). People can't help but be attracted to God when they see believers living in trust and not despair, despite difficult circumstances. Then, as God answers our prayers and works miracles in our lives, we have the opportunity to honor him, thank him, and tell others about his great faithfulness. If we choose to worry and fret instead of trusting the Lord, who gets the glory?

I know, moms tend to worry. It's hard not to. We wring our hands over many issues that are ultimately out of our control. Will our kids succeed in school? Will they get hurt while they are at camp or running on the playground? What if someone is cruel to them? Will they grow

To you, O LORD, I lift up my soul; in you I trust, O my God. —Psalm 25:1–2

up to be honorable and self-reliant adults? We could go on for days with a list of a mother's possible worries! Certainly we must do our best to keep our children safe and to teach and train them properly. We should never confuse casting our cares on the Lord with sitting back and not doing our job. But once we do all that is in our power as mothers to do to take care of our kids, we must leave them—and our worries about them—in God's hands. He is faithful!

Norwegian Christian author O. Hallesby referred to prayer as the "breath of the soul." He wrote:

> The air which our body requires envelops us on every hand. The air of itself seeks to enter our bodies and, for this reason, exerts pressure upon us.... The air which our souls need also envelops all of us at all times and on all sides. God is round about us in Christ on every hand, with His many-sided and all sufficient grace. All we need to do is to open our hearts. Prayer is the breath of the soul, the organ by which we receive Christ into our parched and withered hearts.... As air enters in quietly when we breathe, and does its normal work in our lungs, so Jesus enters quietly into our hearts and does His blessed work there.[4]

Spiritually speaking, we need to breathe continually every day. As we exhale our worries and fears, we inhale the peace of God, knowing that our lives are in his hands. Then we can say with the psalmist, "When I am afraid, I will trust in you. In God, whose word I praise, in God I trust; I will not be afraid. What can mortal man do to me?" (Psalm 56:3–4). And we can stand on the words of Isaiah: "You [the Lord] will keep in perfect peace him whose mind is steadfast, because he trusts in you. Trust in the LORD forever, for the LORD, the LORD, is the Rock eternal" (Isaiah 26:3–4).

As positive Christian moms, we know that we have a solid Rock on whom we can build our lives, and to whom we can entrust our children's lives. Determine to put your confidence and hope in him—and leave your cares far behind.

POWER POINT

Read: Matthew 6:25–34. Underline every instance of the word *worry* in this passage. What does Jesus have to say about worry, and how can you apply those principles to your present anxieties?

Pray: I praise you, for you are a wonderful and caring God. You know my needs before I present them to you. You love me with an everlasting love! Thank you that you care for the needs of the birds of the air, and you care so much more for the needs of my family. I trust you with the worries of my life. I have faith that you are working all things in my life together for the good. Thank you for your abundant love and kindness. In Jesus' name, amen.

Do: Cover a shoebox with wrapping paper, cut a slit in the top, and call it your family's "God Box." Decorate the box with Bible verses such as Philippians 4:6–7; 1 Peter 5:7; Psalm 56:3; and Isaiah 26:3–4. Keep index cards and a pen nearby. Explain to your family members that anytime they are worried about something, they are to write their care on a card and put it in the box as a reminder that they are casting their cares on God. (Make sure you lead by your example!)

Women of Prayer
Changing Lives through the Power of Prayer

*Everyone is capable of praying, but many have the mistaken idea
that they are not called to prayer. Just as we are called to salvation,
we are called to prayer.... Prayer is nothing more than turning our
heart toward God and receiving in turn His love.*
—Jeanne Guyon

Perhaps you remember the "running craze" of the 1980s. I
was a student at Baylor University at the time, and jogging was
quite popular among many of my friends. I wanted to be a runner,
too, but I wasn't sure how to begin. *How does a college girl with no previous experience in track and field become a strong runner?* I wondered. A
friend of mine, a physical education major, gave me this brief but
sound advice: "Just do it." (Apparently, a Nike executive overheard that
conversation!) My friend encouraged me to begin at a slow, steady pace,
be consistent, and stay at it. And you know what? The advice worked!

Since that time, I've been amazed to find that this simple tip can
apply to more areas in life than just running. Take prayer, for example.
How can a mother become a woman of prayer? Just do it! The best way
to learn is to simply begin. Start slow and steady, dedicating just a few
minutes each day to prayer. Then grow from there. As you stay at it,
you will find that a few minutes is no longer enough time to express all
your thanks and lay all your needs before the Lord. By being consistent
in meeting with God each day, you will develop a habit of daily prayer

in your life that will not easily be broken. In fact, you'll find that your prayer time is the key that gives you the power to be a positive mom.

The Power of a Mother's Prayers

Many great and godly women throughout history were praying moms who saw the power of God work through their prayers. How did they become women of prayer? Probably in much the same way that you and I can—by starting with a slow, steady pace that built up to a consistent, daily prayer walk with the Lord. We can learn and draw great encouragement from their examples.

Consider the mother of the great Christian leader Augustine of Hippo. Augustine was born in A.D. 354 to a devout Christian woman named Monica. Monica dearly loved her firstborn son and wholeheartedly believed that God had a plan for his life. But Augustine's father was a pagan man who had little respect for godly moral values, and much to Monica's dismay, Augustine grew up to follow in his father's footsteps. While attending the university in Carthage—a city known for its corruption, brothels, and pagan temples as much as for its learning and culture—Augustine was introduced to skeptical philosophies and a lifestyle of immorality. He even lived with a woman for many years and fathered a child by her, yet couldn't marry her due to the cultural class restrictions.

As you can imagine, Monica grieved and prayed over her son. At one point, seeing little change in Augustine's life or beliefs, she implored a local bishop to talk to her son and help him come to repentance and faith in Christ. But the bishop recognized his limitations; he knew his words could do little to turn a young man's hardened heart. He encouraged Monica to return home and continue in prayer for Augustine. "Go your way, and God bless you," he said, "for it is not possible that the son of these tears should perish."

Monica held on to the bishop's words and continued to plead with God for the salvation of her beloved son. Eventually Augustine's heart began to soften. During a period of doubt and truth-seeking, he decided to give up his pagan beliefs—but stopped short of accepting Christ. Monica continued to pray. Then one day, as Augustine sat in a garden reading from the letters of Paul in the Bible, Monica's prayers came to full fruition. Augustine suddenly realized that these letters from the apostle were meant for him!

To Monica's great joy, Augustine committed the rest of his life to Christ. His own prayer best expressed his mother's response to his new-found faith: "She was jubilant with triumph and glorified you, who are powerful enough, and more than powerful enough, to carry out your purpose beyond all our hopes and dreams."[1]

A similar story is told of John Newton, the wicked sailor of the mid-eighteenth century who later became John Newton, the sailor-preacher. His Christian mother believed in the power of prayer to reform her wayward son. God answered her faithful prayers by changing Newton's heart and lifestyle. He was converted to Christ, and his subsequent preaching and writing reflected his gratitude for God's wonderful salvation. In fact it was Newton, in 1779, who penned the words to "Amazing Grace"—a song that continues to lead people to Christ to this day.[2]

Never underestimate the power of a praying mom! My own mother, Barbara Kinder, was a devoted prayer warrior. She kept a prayer journal, regularly writing out her heartfelt requests to the Father. She and her prayer partner prayed together often, lifting up to God even the smallest details of both families' lives. She prayed for my tests at college, for my dates and friendships, for my running and races. (Yes, my running in college became more than a fad.) She constantly lifted up the minor and the major decisions of my life, praying fervently for

I have many times been driven to my knees by the utter conviction that I had nowhere else to go. —Abraham Lincoln

my future spouse and my career choice. Although I came to faith in Christ at an early age, I am convinced that her prayers kept me on the right path and away from influences that could have set me on a course for destruction.

Busy Moms, Busy Praying

Unfortunately, praying mothers are somewhat of an endangered species these days. When two moms meet—whether at the grocery store, the school parking lot, or the sideline of the soccer field—the typical conversation goes like this: "Hi, how are things going?" "Good, thanks. I've been really busy…" Busy seems to be the name of the game in these fast-paced times. As mothers, we feel that we must always be doing *something*, whether it's church business, work, shopping, volunteering, shuttling kids to activities, or getting together with friends. We seem to think we have an *obligation* to stay busy!

My friend Lisa, the mother of two elementary-age children, made a conscious decision this year not to "overvolunteer" or take on her typical, overflowing plate of outside interests and responsibilities. Bucking all trends, she determined that she would step out of the fast lane for a full twelve months. She is still busy, mind you. But she is busy *praying*.

Yes, praying. Lisa spends a significant amount of time each day praying for the specific needs of her family. She prays for her friends and for the sick and the hurting. She prays for other issues that are brought to her attention. She stands firmly on the promises of God, believing in the power of prayer. She is serious about being busy with the most important business in life: taking her needs—and the needs of her loved ones—to the Father's throne.

In the process, Lisa has *not* become a recluse from life. She has remained involved in her church and her children's school to an extent. But she has chosen to devote most of her energy this year to praying, not running around like the proverbial chicken with its head cut off. I admire her faith and resolve!

Surely the greatest casualty of our overcommitted, warp-speed society is prayer. Fewer mothers these days feel they have time to pray. I can't help but wonder: How different would our homes, our communities, and our churches be if we as mothers did less running around and more praying? What would our country be like right now if thousands upon thousands of prayer-warrior mothers were regularly, fervently lifting up the youth of this nation?

You and I might not be able to make the kind of commitment Lisa has made, but we can find time—*make time*—to lift up the needs of our family, our community, and our nation to God throughout the day. We're busy, it's true. But as François Fenelon wrote, "Time spent in prayer is never wasted."[3]

Becoming a Woman of Prayer

There is no mystery to becoming a woman of prayer. As we said earlier, you just take the first step, then move slowly, steadily, and consistently forward. You pray a few minutes today, then a few minutes tomorrow, then the next day, and the next. God will help you grow from there.

In chapter 6 we talked about the importance of setting aside a place and a time to pray. But once you're in that place, what do you do? Let me say first of all that prayer cannot be reduced to a formula. Conversations with God are too intimate and personal to be "one size fits all." At the same time, certain frameworks for prayer can be helpful tools for those just starting out. One that I recommend is based on the acrostic ACTS.

Principle #2: The Power of Prayer

A—Adoration

Start your prayer time with adoration and praise. In your own words and ways, worship the Lord. Acknowledge his sovereignty and greatness. Tell him how wonderful you believe he is.

C—Confession

Recognizing and praising God's greatness naturally reminds us of our own sinful nature. Take time to humbly confess your sins to God, knowing that when "we confess our sins, he is faithful and just and will forgive us our sins and purify us from all unrighteousness" (1 John 1:9).

T—Thanksgiving

First Thessalonians 5:18 tells us to "give thanks in all circumstances." Yet we so often forget to actually thank God for the things he has done in our lives! Take a few moments to "count your blessings" (as the old hymn goes), then thank God for the love, grace, and mercy he has poured into your life.

S—Supplication

Supplication is the act of telling God our prayer requests—of sharing our needs and the needs of those we love with a loving heavenly Father. Use this part of your prayer time to place all your worries, concerns, and cares in God's all-sufficient hands.

Many moms have found the ACTS acrostic to be a good guideline to follow in their times of prayer. But even with a guideline, we can often feel overwhelmed by the seemingly endless list of things to pray about—our family members, our friends, our church, our pastor, the missionaries we support, our children's school, our job, our local and national governments, and so on. I've personally found it helpful to organize my prayer topics according to the days of the week. This way, I make sure that I pray each week for the people and issues that are on my heart.

Here is a sample plan you might want to adapt for your own purposes:

- Sunday: Pray for your church, its leaders and teachers, and for church leaders around the world.

- Monday: Pray for missionaries around the world, as well as local or national ministries you and your family support.

- Tuesday: Pray for extended family members and in-laws.

- Wednesday: Pray for our government officials and world leaders.

- Thursday: Pray for schools, colleges, institutions, and organizations in which you and your family are involved.

- Friday: Pray for your friends' personal needs.

- Saturday: Pray for the moral integrity of our society. Pray for our nation to have a heart of repentance and a desire to follow God.

Notice that this schedule doesn't include prayer for your children, your spouse, or your personal needs. That's because you will want to be praying for the needs and concerns of your immediate family on a daily basis; the other prayer topics are in addition to these! But whether you use this plan or come up with one of your own, don't forget to record your prayer requests in a prayer journal—and then document God's responses as they come. That way, when you get to that *T* in ACTS, you'll never be at a loss for reasons to say "thank you"!

Partnering in Prayer

Spending time alone with God in prayer is precious and important. But many mothers have found that praying regularly with a special friend—a "prayer partner"—is a wonderful complement to personal prayer. Jesus said, "For where two or three come together in my name, there am I with them" (Matthew 18:20). There is an added strength, a multiplication of faith, that occurs when you and a friend join together on a regular basis to pray over the needs of your families. If you do not already have a friend with whom you can pray, begin now to ask God to bring the right person into your life. Then use these tips to make your prayer times together effective and enjoyable:

1. Be trustworthy. When choosing a prayer partner, make sure she is someone you can trust, since many times your prayers will include deep needs and sensitive family details that shouldn't be shared with the general public. Of course, your partner will be sharing sensitive prayer requests, too. You need to be as trustworthy as you want her to be!

2. Meet regularly. Make every effort to meet with your prayer partner on a regular, scheduled basis. My friend Carol and I meet once a week for prayer. While we are flexible when we need to be (and moms often need to be!), we try to stay as consistent as possible with our weekly prayer times. And on those weeks when we can't meet together face to face, we at least take time to share our prayer needs over the telephone.

3. Write your prayer requests down before you get together. Unfortunately, many women spend most of their time with their prayer partners talking about their problems and trying to solve them—and very little time actually praying about them. By coming to your prayer time with your requests already written down, you can make sure you spend more time praying and less time chatting about the requests.

4. Set a time limit. Make sure you and your prayer partner set a definite starting and stopping time for your meeting together. In this age of busy schedules, just knowing that your prayer time will last a specific length (say, one hour) makes it easier to keep that appointment. If the meetings are always open-ended and frequently go on for hours, however, you may become disheartened and think that you don't really have time for prayer with your partner.

5. Hold one another accountable. A prayer partner can help encourage you to stay committed to prayer—and you can do the same for her. Your enemy, Satan, would love for you to get out of the habit or prayer or to forget about it completely. He knows that you are never so high as when you are on our knees! Your prayer partner can be that external force that holds you accountable and helps you stay steady in prayer.

Chore or Cherished Time?

Can you relate to this mother's prayer?

> Dear Lord, so far today I am doing pretty well. I haven't screamed at the kids or thrown anything in a burst of anger. I have not grumbled or gossiped or whined. I haven't been greedy or self-centered. I have not yet charged anything to the credit card, and I haven't pigged out on the chocolate cake in the refrigerator. However, in a few minutes I will be getting out of bed, and I am going to need your help to make it through the rest of the day. Amen.

The good thing about this mom is that she recognized her need for God's help to make it through the day! She obviously considered prayer a necessity. What is prayer to you? Is it a burden that you must get done each day so you can check it off your "to do" list, or is it a blessed necessity in your life?

Perhaps the following poem by Ralph S. Cushman will provide meaningful motivation as you grow in the blessing of prayer:

The Secret

I met God in the morning
When the day was at its best,
And His presence came like sunrise
Like a glory within my breast.

All day long the presence lingered,
All day long He stayed with me;
And we sailed in perfect calmness
O'er a very troubled sea.

Other ships were blown and battered,
Other ships were sore distressed;
But the winds that seemed to drive them
Brought to us a peace and rest.

Then I thought of other mornings,
With a keen remorse of mind,
When I too had loosed the moorings,
With His presence left behind,

So I think I know the secret
Learned from many a trouble way,
You must seek God in the morning
If you want Him through the day.[4]

Want to be a positive, joyful mom? Then be a praying mom! Jesus stands at the door of our hearts and beckons us: "Until now you have not asked for anything in my name. Ask and you will receive, and your joy will be complete" (John 16:24). By consistently taking our concerns and requests to our heavenly Father, we open the floodgates of God's blessing and joy in our lives and the lives of our family members.

William Law once said, "He who has learned to pray has learned the greatest secret of a holy and a happy life."[5] A positive mom has learned the secret! Each day she meets with her heavenly Father, praising him for who he is—an awesome and wonderful God. She not only asks for help to make it through the day, but also lifts up the needs of her family, her community, and her world. She does not wring her hands in worry but casts her cares daily on the Lord. And as she consistently meets with God day after day after day, a joyful radiance fills her heart, reflected not only in her countenance but in her every word and deed. May you and I learn that secret, too, and grow to be women of faith and prayer!

Power Point

Read: Daniel 6. Notice Daniel's dedication to prayer, even at the risk of death. If Daniel was willing to lose his life for the opportunity to pray, what are you willing to give up in order to have a time of daily prayer?

Pray: O gracious and loving heavenly Father, what a joy and privilege it is to come to you! You are the great Provider, the solid Rock, my faithful Friend. Thank you for hearing my prayers and answering in your time and in your way. My heart and mind are filled with many burdens and needs. I lay them at your feet this moment, knowing you can do all things. I trust you. In Jesus' name I pray. Amen.

Do: Begin today to be a woman of prayer. Spend some quiet time in prayer using the ACTS acrostic (adoration, confession, thanksgiving, and supplication). Ask God to lead you to a faithful and trustworthy friend with whom you can pray on a regular basis. Remain committed to your time with your prayer partner for at least six weeks to form the habit of praying together.

Principle #3

THe Pwer OF A Good Attitude

Do everything without complaining or arguing.
—Philippians 2:14

Constant complaint is the poorest sort of pay
for all the comforts we enjoy.
—Benjamin Franklin

The Ladies Pity Party
Don't Accept the Invitation

I have learned to be content whatever the circumstances.
I know what it is to be in need, and I know what it is to have plenty.
I have learned the secret of being content in any and every situation,
whether well fed or hungry, whether living in plenty or in want.
I can do everything through him who gives me strength.
—Philippians 4:11–13

As the author of several party books, I am often invited to speak to women's groups on the topic of how to plan memorable parties. Women love parties—birthday parties, baby showers, wedding showers, anniversary parties, holiday parties, all kinds of parties! But the one party that tends to attract the most women, particularly in North America, is the Ladies Pity Party. The invitation goes something like this:

> You are cordially invited to self-indulge in
> A Pity Party
> Place: *At home or at meetings or gatherings with friends*
> Date and Time: *Any time, any day*
> Please Bring: *A spirit of discontentment, complaints*
> *of every kind, a negative attitude, plus a detailed list of*
> *everything that is wrong with your life*
> RSVP: *to your conscience (only if declining)*

Take my advice: Don't accept the invitation! I know life is not always fair. It's not always easy, especially for mothers. But you and I have a choice each day whether to wallow in self-pity or put our trust in God as he works in our lives.

What do moms tend to whine about? For starters, the laundry, the dishes, the clutter. Then we expand our complaining to include our husband's shortcomings and our children's squabbles. Finally we look outside the home to grumble about the neighbors, the teachers at our children's school, and problems at our church. There is never a shortage of subject matter for a good pity party! The question we face day by day, even moment by moment, is whether or not we will attend.

Why do we complain? One reason, I think, is because complaining is easy! It is simple to say what is wrong about a situation; it's more difficult to find what is right and talk about the good points. Another reason is that we tend to find fellowship in common complaints. When we have something negative to converse about, we can talk for hours—why something's bad, how it might get worse, how my bad circumstance compares to your bad circumstance, and so on.

A third reason we complain is to get attention. It's not always popular to sound like a Pollyanna, pointing out the positive. But when we sing that all-too-familiar tune, "Nobody knows the trouble I've seen," our friends rush to our side to give us sympathy for our pain. Of course, they fully expect that sympathy to be reciprocated when it's their turn to whine!

Checking Your Focus

Grumbling is an age-old problem, not just a modern vice. The Israelites, for example, had a real problem with complaining when they left behind their four-hundred-year bondage in Egypt to follow Moses out into the wilderness. They complained about the lack of water, so God provided water. They complained about the food, so God gave them manna from heaven. They wailed about their lack of meat, so

God sent them quail. They continued to grumble and complain about their hardships (poor Moses!)—even saying that they'd be better off back in Egypt as slaves.

Had God left them for a moment? No. Were they starving for lack of provisions? No. The Bible even says that the shoes on their feet did not wear out during their journey in the wilderness! So how did God feel about their groaning? Numbers 11:1–2 gives us a picture:

> Now the people complained about their hardships in the hearing of the LORD, and when he heard them his anger was aroused. Then fire from the LORD burned among them and consumed some of the outskirts of the camp. When the people cried out to Moses, he prayed to the LORD and the fire died down.

Oh my! Apparently, God was not at all pleased with the Israelites' constant complaining. Can we blame him? He had miraculously delivered the Israelites from slavery in Egypt. He was lovingly leading them toward the Promised Land. Along the way, he was providing for all of their needs. Yet they still complained! Granted, their journey was hard, and their wilderness camp was no luxury resort. But instead of focusing on the great miracles God had done on their behalf and his goodness toward them in securing their freedom, they focused on what was bad about the situation.

Aren't you glad God doesn't send down fire on our camps today? Many of our yards would be burning! The truth is every coin has two sides, an upside and a downside. Most circumstances in our lives have two sides as well. Are we able to see God's provision for us? Do we see his hand at work for our good? Or are we so focused on our problems that all we can do is complain?

Perhaps you are saying, "But you don't know how bad my circumstances are." You're right! I don't know what you are going through. But

I do know there are women who are probably in far worse situations, yet they are making it through the tough times without drowning in self-pity. I also know there are women with relatively minimal challenges in their lives who still grumble every step of the way—making life miserable for themselves and for everyone around them.

The question is not "What are you going through?" but "What is your perspective and attitude in the process?" As you may know, the famous author Robert Louis Stevenson was bedridden with tuberculosis for much of his life. One day, he began to hack and cough loudly. His wife said to him, "I suppose you still believe it is a wonderful day." Stevenson turned toward his window where the bright yellow sunshine blazed through and said, "I do! I will never let a row of medicine bottles block my horizon."[1]

Are you looking at the sunshine—or the medicine bottles? Don't let anything block your horizon! The Bible says, "Let us fix our eyes on Jesus, the author and perfecter of our faith, who for the joy set before him endured the cross" (Hebrews 12:2). Jesus was able to endure more than you and I will ever have to—all because he had his eyes focused on the joy of securing our salvation. If we are going to be positive moms, we need to check our focus. Dr. Laura Schlessinger puts it simply: "Stop whining!"

The Secret of Contentment

The story is told of a king who was glum and discontent. No matter what he did, he just couldn't seem to get out of his sad state. Finally, he called his wise men together and asked for help. The men conferred, then approached the king with their remedy.

"O king, if you will wear the shirt of a contented man, you too will be content," they said. So the king immediately sent out search parties from the castle to travel throughout the land, looking for a man who was truly content. For months, the king's representatives traveled far and wide. They looked among the nobility, then among the villagers, then among the commoners. Finally after nearly a year of searching, the announcement came from a far corner of the kingdom: "We have found a contented man!"

The king sent a reply: "Hurry, get me his shirt!"

Sometime later, another message arrived at the castle. "Sire, we have searched the countryside for a contented man, and we have found him," it read. "But alas, he has no shirt!"

The man didn't even have a shirt on his back, yet he was content! How could this be? The truth is, contentment comes from the heart; it is not dependent on material things. Are you waiting on an updated kitchen or new wall-to-wall carpet to be content? Do you think that if your kids get into the best schools you will be happy? Are you waiting for the day when your husband is more sensitive and understanding of your feelings? Why wait? The truth is, our contentment is independent of what we have or who surrounds us.

Contentment is the opposite of self-pity. If our hearts are content because we trust in God as our loving provider, then we'll tend to keep our eyes off our troubles. But if we dwell on our wants or our difficulties (great or small), we will lose sight of the provisions God is granting us.

The Old Testament character Job learned this secret of contentment. Amazingly, after losing everything—his home, his wealth, his family, even his health—he was able to say, "Naked I came from my mother's womb, and naked I will depart. The LORD gave and the LORD has taken away; may the name of the LORD be praised" (Job 1:21). In all of his sorrows, Job continued to believe in God's goodness. He refused to charge God with wrongdoing, even when his complaining wife urged him, "Curse God and die!" (Job 2:9). Job resisted the temptation to be

He is richest who is content with the least. —Charles H. Spurgeon

The real voyage of discovery consists not in seeking new landscapes but in having new eyes. —Marcel Proust

angry with God. He knew his peace and security came not from having a multitude of things, but from knowing beyond a shadow of a doubt that God was faithful.

Our church in North Dallas helps with a wonderful ministry called Voice of Hope that provides an after-school program in a Christian environment for underprivileged kids. Several years ago my family, along with others, agreed to help deliver holiday turkey dinners to some of the families that were being served by Voice of Hope. Our simple task was to deliver the dinners to the people's homes and sing a few Christmas carols.

At virtually every house, we were greeted by wonderfully warm and grateful people. Each visit went the same way: We presented the dinners, sang our songs (even though none of us could carry a tune), then said our good-byes. To my surprise, almost every household asked if they could offer a prayer before we left. Their prayers typically went something like this:

> Dear Lord, you have given us so very much. We do not deserve your rich blessings! Thank you, Lord Jesus. Thank you for your loving-kindness, your forgiveness, and your mercy. Thank you most of all for your son, Jesus, in whom we have abundant life. Thank you also for these kind people who have brought us a bountiful turkey dinner. We are so grateful! In your wonderful son's name we pray. Amen.

These were contented people! They had very little in the way of possessions, but they were rich with peace and joyfulness. My family and the other volunteers learned an incredible lesson that day as we got back in our SUVs and returned to overindulgent, discontent North Dallas. We learned that contentment is not based on what you have; it is based on how you choose to view life. It is an issue of the heart.

Paul's Potential Pity Party

Consider the apostle Paul for a moment. Now, here was a man who deserved a pity party! He was thrown into a Roman prison not for committing a terrible crime, but for sharing the gospel of Jesus throughout Asia Minor. Certainly he could have whined, shaken his fist at God, and cried, "It's not fair!" We wouldn't have blamed him, would we? Haven't we all said those words at some time in our lives?

Many situations in life are not fair, especially for mothers. We work hard serving our families and the needs of our homes, and we don't get enough appreciation for all we do. It's not fair! Paul could have said the same thing. "I've given my all to tell others about Jesus, and what has it gotten me? A jail cell!" Paul could have grumbled and complained and given up on the mission God had called him to. But he didn't.

Instead, Paul faced this challenging situation by choosing to look up and not down. He did not focus on how bad the circumstances were but on what could God do through the circumstances. And what did God do? For one, he opened up many opportunities for Paul to minister to the prison guards, the officials who tried him, and the visitors who came to see him each day. Second, he made sure Paul had some ink and some papyrus and prompted him to begin writing. Today we can open our New Testaments and refer to the letters Paul wrote to the early churches from his prison cell. We can see—and benefit from—the awesome work that God did through Paul in prison.

Paul was able to write these words during his time in jail: "I have learned to be content whatever the circumstances" (Philippians 4:11). Now if Paul could say this from his prison cell, I wonder if we could say it from our laundry room? The good news is that Paul did not leave any confusion as to how he was able to be content. In the next two verses he gives us the key that unlocks the prison door of self-pity: "I know what it is to be in need, and I know what it is to have plenty. I have learned the secret of being content in any and every situation, whether well fed or hungry, whether living in plenty or in want. *I can do everything through him who gives me strength*" (vv. 12–13, emphasis added).

Perhaps you have heard that last phrase before. You may have even memorized it in another translation: "I can do all things through Christ who strengthens me" (NKJV). It is truly a wonderful—but often misused—verse. Did you realize that Paul was talking about contentment when he wrote it? He was giving us the key to unlocking our prison of self-pity: believing that with God's strength, we can get through whatever life brings.

Can we still be content if our child doesn't get the best teacher in the first grade? If our friend disappoints us? If our husband won't agree to new carpet for the living room? Through all the stressful and challenging situations of life, we can still find contentment when we fix our eyes and place our hope in God—the only one who can give us strength to make it through.

Heading Off Bitterness and Anger

When we forget that key to contentment, we can spend all of our time dwelling on the negative in situations—and that's dangerous. When we continue to rehearse our discontented thoughts and attitudes over and over, anger and bitterness set in, threatening and sometimes destroying the relationships we hold most dear.

Recently our family took a cruise to the Caribbean. We enjoyed visiting many wonderful tropical islands and seeing the sights as our large ship sailed from port to port. Standing on the deck one afternoon, we watched in awe as smoke billowed out of a mountain on the nearby island of Montserrat. We realized we were looking at an active volcano. What an impressive sight!

That volcano comes to mind as I think about the danger of anger in relationships. As it rumbles within us and heats up over time, anger can erupt and overflow. And just as the hot lava of a volcano destroys everything in its path, so our outbursts of anger, rooted in resentment, bitterness, and self-pity, can destroy the people around us.

I think about Suzette, who married a wonderful man but was discontent from the moment she returned from the honeymoon. She didn't feel that her husband's job provided her with the income she desired. The home he could afford wasn't in the "right" neighborhood. He never seemed to help out enough around the house and with the kids. And he certainly wasn't sensitive to her feelings!

Over time, the bitterness and anger festered and grew inside of her. What began as a spirit of discontent led Suzette to begin looking for greener grass—and eventually to an affair with her husband's best friend, Rick. The devastation and heartache caused to both families has been incalculable. If only Suzette's discontentment had been checked at the door of her heart before she began each day, perhaps this picture would have turned out differently!

How do you keep anger from overtaking your heart? You cut it off at the pass! Here are three simple steps you can follow daily:

1. Recognize who the enemy is. This is the first step in any successful battle plan. Your real enemy is Satan, who would like nothing more than for you to get your eyes off God and onto your problems. What are the areas about which you tend to complain? These are the places where Satan will try to get a foothold. Make a mental boundary around these areas and put up a sign that says "No Self-Pity Allowed."

2. Change your perspective. Consider what is good about your situation. Write it down. In every situation there are positives, although they

Happiness is a habit—cultivate it. —Elbert Hubbard

☺

may be hard to see. If you cannot see any positives, then hold on to this one fact: God loves you and will be with you through the difficulties.

3. Ask God to give you strength. Pray to God for strength based on Philippians 4:11–13. Ask him to dismantle your discontented spirit and replace it with a peace that "transcends all understanding" (Philippians 4:7). Thank God for his provisions for you and your family.

Rising above the Fray

Imagine a wonderful day you have planned for your kids. You feed them a nutritious breakfast, complete with eggs, ham, whole-wheat pancakes, and fresh-squeezed orange juice. They respond by complaining about the temperature of the eggs, the texture of "those healthy pancakes," and the orange pulp on the sides of their glasses. Next you take them out to their favorite park. They whine because you won't let them play in the creek and get soaked. Afterward, you go to the library for story time, but the kids frown and grumble and refuse to sit still. Finally, you drop by the grocery store to pick up their favorite food for dinner, and they cry, "We don't want to go in! We want to go home! It's not fair!"

By dinnertime, you are no doubt exhausted! Here you are, trying to do what is best for your children from sunup to sundown, and all they do is complain!

Believe me, God understands. His children frequently complain and grumble and whine, oblivious to all the good he is doing in their lives. May you and I not be those kinds of kids!

Instead, as positive moms with children of our own, let's determine to decline the daily invitation to the Ladies Pity Party. Yes, situations may not always go as we would like. Life may throw us some curves. But through it all we know that we have a loving heavenly Father, and we can rest assured that he is providing for all our needs.

POWER POINT

Read: Philippians 4. Which verses help you to be a more positive person? Memorize verse 8 as an invitation to a Positive Party and not a Pity Party.

Pray: I praise you, wonderful Father, for you are able to provide for all of my needs. Thank you that you are the Good Shepherd. You lovingly tend me and my family as a good shepherd would take care of his sheep. Thank you not only for the green pastures in my life, but the deserts I must journey through as well. I am confident you will never leave me. Help me to be a positive woman, looking for the good in every situation you allow in my life. Help me to decline the opportunity to feel sorry for myself. Give me strength to live this life abundantly and victoriously. In Jesus' name, amen.

Do: Hang a wall calendar in your kitchen. On the square with today's date, write one thing that you can think of that is good about this day. Then with each passing day, write a new entry in the appropriate square. At the end of the month you will have a calendar full of good perspectives and positive thoughts gleaned from the month. Make it a daily habit to find what is good about the day!

Attitude of Gratitude
Creating a Thankful Environment

Come let us sing for joy to the LORD: let us shout
aloud to the Rock of our salvation.
Let us come before him with thanksgiving
and extol him with music and song.
—Psalm 95:1–2

Few activities are more delightful than watching children, wide-eyed with excitement and wonder, opening brightly wrapped gifts on Christmas morning. Two types of children generally emerge under the Christmas tree. First there are the grateful ones—those kids who react with gratitude as they open every package, even if they don't like the present or already have two of the same thing. Then there are the difficult-to-please ones—those kids who respond with a less-than-enthusiastic "oh, thanks" as they open each box with thinly veiled disappointment. Even when kids in this second group get something they want, it never seems to be quite right! "Uh, nice wagon. Didn't they have a red one?" "I wanted a new dress…this one looks a little big."

Now, which of these two types of children do you think enjoy their Christmas most? Surely the first group! It's amazing how attitude makes all the difference—and not just on Christmas morning. This scene around the Christmas tree is but a brief snapshot of the big picture of life. Some people view life through the eyes of thankfulness; others dwell on the negatives. Of the two groups, thankful people are happier people.

Principle #3: The Power of a Good Attitude

I know a woman—let's call her Brenda—who always has a smile on her face. She is a bright light to everyone around her! Many people would be disappointed and angry if they had been given her lot in life, but not Brenda; she is a thankful person. After trying to have children for years, Brenda finally received a phone call informing her that the test results were positive. She was pregnant! But her excitement was mixed with concern about how her husband would receive this information. Their marriage was already shaky, and when she broke the news, her husband was less than thrilled. They divorced soon after the baby was born.

Brenda was faced with the prospect of raising a son on her own. Her ex-husband refused to pay child support, making her situation even more difficult. Brenda knew she had a choice: Would she become angry and bitter, or would she look for the good in the situation? Brenda decided to be a thankful person. She gave thanks to God for the gift of her wonderful son. She gave thanks for her God-given talents that enabled her to earn money to support her little family. She thanked the Lord for her parents, who moved close by to help. With a thankful heart, she chose to look for the loving hand of God in the situation and refused to allow angry and bitter thoughts to fester.

Several years later, Brenda received the terrible news that her brother had suddenly died of an undetected heart problem. Her entire family, which had always been very close, was devastated. But even through this sad and difficult time, Brenda had peace, knowing that her brother was in heaven and God was with them both. She was able to give thanks for the years she had been blessed to spend with her brother.

That event actually became something of a turning point for Brenda. Realizing that time is precious, she began to reexamine her schedule, consider her priorities, and change her life accordingly. She

A grateful mind is both a great and happy mind. —William Secker

wasn't thankful for her brother's death, of course, but she was thankful for what God was able to do through the situation. Today Brenda is a positive mom because she is a thankful mom. She continues to choose to view life's challenges through gratitude-colored glasses.

What glasses do you use to view the world? Are they rosy, gratitude-colored glasses that help you look at your circumstances through the eyes of faith, trusting that God will see you through? Or are they dark-shaded glasses that block out your view of the Son, allowing you to see only what is wrong with a situation?

Ultimately the quality of your life and mine depends on the way we view it. Bible teacher Chuck Swindoll puts it this way:

> The longer I live, the more I realize the impact of attitude on life. Attitude, to me, is more important than facts. It is more important than the past, than money, than circumstances, than failures, than success, than what other people think or say or do. It is more important than appearance, giftedness or skill. It will make or break a company...a church...a home, or an individual. The remarkable thing is we have a choice every day regarding the attitude we will embrace for that day. We cannot change our past...we cannot change the fact that people will act in a certain way. We cannot change the inevitable. The only thing we can do is play on the one string we have, and that is our attitude. I am convinced that life is ten percent what happens to me and ninety percent how I react to it. And so it is with you...we are in charge of our attitudes.[1]

Each day Brenda chooses to have an attitude of gratitude, impacting not only her own life but the lives of her family members and friends. She is a beacon of blessing and joy to everyone she knows. Would someone say the same about you and me?

Giving Thanks in Everything

I know it's not always easy to be thankful. Sometimes we have to look long and hard for the smallest spark of something to be thankful for. At times we must simply trust God, knowing that every circumstance that comes into our lives was first filtered through his loving hands. The essence of faith is being able to say, "Thank you, God," in every situation, even when we don't see anything good about it.

The apostle Paul (writing from the confines of a prison cell) tells us to "give thanks in all circumstances" (1 Thessalonians 5:18). How can we do this? Only by putting our faith in the goodness of God's character and trusting in his love for us. We can give thanks in everything, Paul says, "for this is God's will for you in Christ Jesus" (v. 18). It's hard to believe that the difficult times are a part of God's loving will. But the Bible is clear: Even through life's difficulties, "God works for the good of those who love him, who have been called according to his purpose" (Romans 8:28). There is always something to be thankful for!

As moms, we have many reasons to give thanks—if we will just open our eyes and see them. That's the message behind this prayer of gratitude written by my friend Anne:

A Mother's Thankful Heart

I come before You Father
To thank You for this life
The blessings You have given me
As a mother and a wife

I'm thankful for my children
As I watch them grow and play

134

Knowing that each moment
Will live for just today

I'm thankful for the laundry
For the dust to wipe away
I'm thankful for the problems
That make me stop and pray

I'm thankful for my husband's job
The roof above our heads
I'm thankful for our daily food
For the comfort of our beds

I'm thankful for the errands
The phone that always rings
I'm thankful for the tears we cry
For the joy that laughter brings

I'm thankful for our family's love
The way we sit and talk
The simple games we often play
The picnics and the walks

I'm thankful for the little things
That make up every day
For therein lies Your love, Lord
And the wonder of Your ways

I'm thankful for the memories
That life has brought my way
I count it as Your blessing
To be a mother every day[2]

Have you ever stopped in the midst of your daily routine just to offer a prayer of thanksgiving? Let's try an experiment. Stop reading, put this book down, and take a moment to thank the Lord for at least three blessings in your life. There now, doesn't that feel good? I bet you didn't stop at three things!

Unfortunately, many people forget to express their gratitude—even when their blessings are more obvious than a sink full of dirty dishes. The story of the ten lepers in Luke 17 is a perfect example. The Bible says that ten men, suffering from the dreadful, disfiguring disease of leprosy, approached Jesus and asked for healing. In his compassion, Jesus told them to go show themselves to the priests. As they obediently walked on their way, they found they had been miraculously healed!

Yet, amazingly, only one of the healed men came back to say, "Thank you." Jesus asked him, "Were not all ten cleansed? Where are the other nine? Was no one found to return and give praise to God?" (v. 17). Only one out of ten made the effort to express gratitude!

As positive moms, we must never become like those nine ungrateful people who received a life-changing gift from God but forgot to return and say, "Thank you." Instead, we must take time each day to give thanks for all of God's blessings. For me, that time is often when I lay my head on my pillow at night and think over the events and the blessings of the day. I find that when I put my mind to it, I begin to see all sorts of reasons to give thanks that I never saw before. Try it yourself tonight. It's a wonderful way to go to sleep—with a grateful heart!

Gratitude Is Contagious

We can give our children no greater gift than a positive, consistent attitude of gratitude. Attitudes are contagious! If we are discontented, our kids know it and begin to reflect it. If we are grateful, they pick up on that too. What attitudes are our kids catching from us? If we are making the effort to develop a habit of giving thanks, our kids will grow up to be thankful as well.

I've found that the dinner table is a great place to begin teaching children about thankfulness. As you offer thanks for the meal, go ahead and mention several other things for which you and you family can be thankful. Later, as you put your kids to bed at night, take another opportunity to thank God, spotlighting in prayer the good things he is doing in their lives and yours.

You might also want to start a "Grateful Poster" in your kids' rooms to help them reflect on God's loving-kindness toward them. Have your children help you decorate a poster board using stickers and markers. Add some sequins and glitter for an extra flair. Then work with your kids to come up with a small sentence each day that thanks God for his blessings, both great and small. Older kids can decorate a bulletin board and tack up notes of thanks to God. These visual reminders will help keep your children's thoughts in a thankful direction and hopefully instill a habit of thankfulness in their lives.

In the utility room in our house, we have a large chalkboard that is seen by every family member at one time or another during the day. I write funny quotes, interesting sayings, and important messages to my family on this board. Now and then I simply write at the top "I am thankful for…" and leave the rest of the board blank. I encourage Curt and the girls to fill in the blank in different colors of chalk. It is always fun and informative to see what everyone has written by the end of the day.

Pollyanna Was Right

Perhaps you are familiar with the story of Pollyanna, which was made into a wonderful movie by that name back in 1960. The main character, played by a young Hayley Mills, was a delightful little girl who came to live with her rich but dour Aunt Polly following the death of her missionary parents. Pollyanna ended up bringing joy and happiness to Aunt Polly's otherwise gloomy household.

Give thanks in all circumstances, for this is God's will for you in Christ Jesus. —1 Thessalonians 5:18

Little Pollyanna played a game that gave her a unique outlook on life: the Glad Game. Whenever she was feeling down, she would try to think of something to be glad about. She explained that the game was first started by her parents on the foreign mission field. Pollyanna had been anxiously waiting for a special doll that was supposed to come in a large missionary shipment. But when the barrel arrived from overseas, there was no doll—only a pair of child-sized crutches with a note attached explaining, "There hadn't been any dolls come in, but the little crutches had." The note went on to suggest that perhaps some poor child could use them.

To help Pollyanna deal with her disappointment, her father instituted the Glad Game at that moment. He encouraged his daughter to find something to be glad about in the situation. Pollyanna finally realized that she could be glad simply because she didn't have to use the crutches![3]

Some people get annoyed when others consistently respond to complaints or grumpiness with positive, rosy comments—but not our heavenly Father. He wants us to practice an attitude of gratitude, giving thanks in everything. He knows a thankful attitude is good for us and for the people around us. And as is often the case, science is now catching up with God. Doctors and researchers are beginning to recognize the clear health benefits of focusing on the good. The prestigious Stanford Health Care Center has even begun offering a workshop with the title "Happiness: Pollyanna Was Right!"[4]

We can play the Glad Game as positive mothers in our homes. When the milk spills, we can be glad the glass didn't break. When it's raining and the kids can't play outside, we can be glad to have a day to snuggle with them and read or play an indoor game. When a child brings home a bad grade on a math test, we can be glad there will be another chance to do better. It's not always easy to come up with some-

The man who forgets to be grateful has fallen asleep in life. —Robert Louis Stevenson

thing to be glad about, but playing the Glad Game forces us to have a positive outlook on life.

Of course, we must be sensitive to sad feelings. If a child is truly upset about something, that may not be the best moment to point out a reason to be glad. Remember what Romans 12:15 tells us: "Rejoice with those who rejoice; mourn with those who mourn." There are times when the Glad Game doesn't fit the circumstances. But more often than not, making the effort to think positive thoughts will help us avoid frustration and embrace thankfulness, even in difficult situations.

The story is told of a little boy named Tommy who tried out for a part in the school play. He had his heart so set on being in the program that his mother, quite aware of his lack of acting talent, feared that he would be crushed when he wasn't chosen. On the day the roles were announced, Tommy's mother made sure she was first in the carpool line so she'd be able to console him right away if he was upset. To her surprise, Tommy came rushing out of school toward her car, his face beaming. "Mommy, mommy!" he shouted. "I have been chosen to clap and cheer!"

When it comes to being thankful, perspective is everything. Let's be positive moms and show our families the blessing of having an attitude of gratitude.

POWER POINT

Read: Three women's songs of thanks to God: Hannah's (1 Samuel 2:1–10), Deborah's (Judges 5:1–31), and Mary's (Luke 1:46–55). Notice how these women recognized God's handiwork in their lives and took the time to offer thanks.

Pray: Thank you, Father, for your mercy, your forgiveness, and your loving care for me. Thank you for my family—for every good and not-so-good quality in each member. Thank you for the privilege of being a mother! Thank you for the circumstances in my life this very moment; help me to see your hand at work. In Jesus' name, amen.

☺ **Do:** Start a Thanksgiving Journal. Using a blank notebook, begin recording your prayers of thanks to God. Make it a habit to write in the journal on a regular basis, whether once a day, once a week, or once a month. Now and then reflect on past prayers of thanks, remembering what God has done in your life. You may even want to read some of the prayers to your kids, especially the prayers that concern them.

The Challenges of Life
Learning to Grow through Difficult Circumstances

For every hill I've had to climb, For every stone that bruised my feet,
For all the blood and sweat and grime,
For blinking storms and burning heat,
My heart sings but a grateful song—
These were the things that made me strong!
—Anonymous

Wilma Rudolph was born prematurely and faced numerous complications. She developed double pneumonia (twice) and scarlet fever, and later had a bout with polio that left her with a crooked leg and a foot that twisted inward. As a result, Wilma endured her childhood with her legs in braces—an adversity that built a determined spirit within her. At the age of eleven she began slipping the braces off and secretly attempting to walk without them. Finally the doctor gave his consent to allow Wilma to remove the braces at times. This, to Wilma, meant never putting them on again.

At the age of thirteen, with much hard work and perseverance, Wilma made her school basketball and track teams. At sixteen, she reached the semifinals in the 200-meter dash in the 1956 Olympic Games. She came home with a bronze metal as a member of the 400-meter relay team.

Wilma committed herself to returning to the 1960 Olympics for a gold medal and immediately began a rigorous and disciplined training program. While putting in numerous hours at the track, she also paid her way through Tennessee State University, maintaining the B average that was required to stay on the track team. Her hard work was rewarded. At the 1960 Olympics, she came through victoriously with three gold medals—the first American woman to win three gold medals in track and field in a single Olympics.[1]

Challenges? Yes, Wilma Rudolph had many challenges in life; but instead of letting them get her down, she was determined to overcome them. Difficulties in life are inevitable for all of us. The question is, what will we do with them?

If Only…

Just as a precious stone can only be polished with friction, so our lives are perfected through the trials and challenges that come our way. If we had our choice, we'd probably choose to go through life without any struggles. Who wouldn't want life to be easier? But like it or not, our struggles actually serve a purpose. They help us grow and develop into stronger, wiser, and more faithful people.

How would you fill in the following blank? "Life would be more enjoyable if only _____." What is the problem or difficulty, great or small, that you'd most like to see go away? If only…

…we didn't live in this neighborhood.

…my husband had a better job or made more money or worked harder.

…I didn't have all this laundry to do.

…my child was more compliant.

…my house was bigger.

…the kids wouldn't fight.

…my child had a better teacher.

…my parents lived nearby.

…his parents lived out of town.

What did you put in the blank? Whatever it was, stop right now and take a few moments to ask God to help you make it through that circumstance. Ask him to help you find something to be thankful for in the situation. Then promise that you will never say "if only" again, for those words only serve to send your heart and mind reeling in a negative direction. "If only" makes you look backward with regret, focusing your thoughts on things you can not change, rather than looking forward to what God can do in and through the struggle. A friend of mine puts it this way: "Every time I face a challenge, whether great or small, I look at it as an opportunity to trust God."

Moses was a man who refused to say "if only." He faced many setbacks in his life, any one of which could have been the "final straw" that would have rendered him helpless. Yet for Moses, each challenge turned into a new opportunity to allow God to work through him as the leader of the Israelites. From being saved as a baby from the murderous pharaoh, to fleeing Egypt and living in the desert for forty years, to leading millions of people across the dry bed of the Red Sea, Moses was a man who faced many challenges. But instead of regretting what he couldn't change, Moses looked at the difficulties as opportunities to see God's hand at work.

As we peer through the portholes of time we find numerous examples of heroes, leaders, writers, composers, and inventors who overcame great hurdles in their lives and were better men and women as a result. Take, for example, Ludwig van Beethoven (1770–1827). By the age of thirty, Beethoven was stone deaf, yet he was still able to compose his greatest work. Beethoven's *Ninth Symphony*, which many consider to be his greatest, combined instruments and voices in a majestic expression of glorious sound. Perhaps you have heard the touching story of the first performance of the *Ninth Symphony* in Vienna, Austria, in 1824. Beethoven was unaware of the thunderous applause he was given by the audience until the soloist came down from the stage and turned him around to see the cheering.[2]

Have courage for the great sorrows of life and patience for the small ones. And when you have finished your daily task, go to sleep in peace. God is awake. —Victor Hugo

Fanny Crosby (1820–1915) is another example. Blinded at a young age due to improper medical treatment, she received her education from the New York School for the Blind and served as a teacher there. In 1858 she married Alexander Van Alstyne, a blind musician and one of the school's music teachers. She began writing verses for secular songs but turned to writing gospel lyrics in her early forties. She never wrote lyrics for a hymn without first kneeling in prayer and asking for God's guidance. Over the course of her lifetime, she wrote more than eight thousand songs, including "Blessed Assurance," "Rescue the Perishing," and "All the Way My Savior Leads Me."[3]

What are the challenges you face in your life? Whatever comes your way, you can be sure that God is with you—even through the lowest points. I love this passage from Isaiah 43:1–2:

> Fear not, for I have redeemed you;
> I have summoned you by name; you are mine.
> When you pass through the waters, I will be with you;
> And when you pass through the rivers, they will not sweep over you.
> When you walk through the fire, you will not be burned; the
> flames will not set you ablaze.
> For I am the LORD, your God,
> The Holy One of Israel, your Savior.

Sooner or later we will all face a crisis. We will all experience our own personal fire or flood. "In this world you will have trouble," Jesus said in John 16:33—not as a promise but as a reality check. Your crisis may be a life-changing event; it may be a minor blip on the big screen of life. You may feel like you're drowning at this very moment. But whatever difficulty you face, you can have faith that God is there with you. You can trust that he will use the struggle to help you grow stronger, both as a woman and as a mother.

Strength in the Struggle

The story is told of an old man who discovered a caterpillar. He decided to keep the small creature and watch its transformation into a butterfly. Sure enough, within days the fuzzy worm began spinning its cocoon. The man watched with fascination as the entire encasement was meticulously completed. Then he waited. And waited.

Finally, after several weeks, the old man noticed that the butterfly was beginning to emerge from its woven shell. His interest turned to concern, however, as he watched the little creature struggling hard to free itself. Feeling compassion, he decided to help. With a small knife he clipped away part of the cocoon, enabling the butterfly to get out quickly and easily. But the man's initial delight turned to sorrow as he saw the beautiful creature now struggle to fly. You see, butterflies strengthen their wings through the process of pushing and struggling against the cocoon walls. As they emerge, fluid is pushed from their bodies into their wings, giving them the necessary elements to fly. In cutting away the cocoon, the man had denied the butterfly the opportunity it needed to persevere and grow strong on its own.

Sometimes we, as mothers, treat our children like that old man treated the butterfly. We do everything we can to help them avoid struggle. We shield them from sadness, disappointment, and the challenges of life. No mother wants to see her children sad or disappointed, of course; but the truth is, it is neither healthy nor beneficial to prevent our kids from going through challenges. How else will they grow strong? How else will they develop the faith they'll need to survive the inevitable storms of life? How else will they learn to approach God as their "refuge and strength, an ever-present help in trouble" (Psalm 46:1)?

At my children's school I've noticed that there are three types of mothers. Some mothers hover like helicopters over their children, trying to make sure their kids get the best teachers, the best grades, the best roles in the school play, even the best seats in the lunchroom. Others say (in actions, if not words), "I don't care what you do, kids. You are on your own"—and they keep their distance from most school activities. Then there are those mothers who walk in faith, assisting their children when it's appropriate but allowing them to experience struggle and disappointment too.

Several years ago a particular teacher at school—I'll call her Mrs. Tobin—had a reputation for being difficult and not always kind to her students. Few parents would choose to have their child in her class. Of course, the helicopter moms met with the principal before the school year started to ensure that their children would not be in this woman's classroom. Other parents didn't care. Still others simply trusted God and the school officials to do what was best for their kids.

When my daughter reached Mrs. Tobin's grade level, I decided not to approach the principal. To that point, I had made it a personal policy not to interfere with the choice of my children's teachers. I knew that the administrators and teachers carefully and prayerfully considered the placement of the students each year. And as you can probably guess, my daughter ended up in *her* class.

At the beginning of the school year, my daughter was less than thrilled to have Mrs. Tobin as her teacher. But as we talked about the situation, I encouraged her to see it as an opportunity to trust God and to learn to understand and work with "difficult people." While some kids were being shielded from that struggle, I explained, the students in Mrs. Tobin's class would learn to deal with challenges—and grow and mature in the process. They would learn that they didn't have to fear difficult situations, because God was able to give them the grace and the help they needed to make it through.

One day my daughter came home from school and told me that

Mrs. Tobin had shared some of her personal struggles with the class that day. She had confessed to the students that her attitude had been less than loving, and she was now asking God to help her be a kinder and gentler person. What a great lesson that turned out to be! Mrs. Tobin's students not only were given the opportunity to watch and experience the grace of God working in their teacher's life; they were allowed to see an example of an open, honest woman who was willing to be vulnerable enough to share her struggles with others. And if God could do a miracle in Mrs. Tobin's life, then surely he could do miracles in their lives too!

I'm glad I didn't try to shield my daughter from her initial discomfort and cause her to miss that lesson and many others she learned that year in Mrs. Tobin's class.

We hurt our children and block God's work when we protect them from difficulties and disappointments in life. The truth is, life will not always go the way we want it to. And if we aren't willing to persevere, adjust, and grow, we might just miss some special blessings that God has prepared for us. As the old saying goes, if you want to see a rainbow, you must first experience some rain!

I like the approach to adversity that Emily Perl Kingsley takes in her story "Welcome to Holland," which was published in the book *Chicken Soup for the Mother's Soul:*

I am often asked to describe the experience of raising a child with a disability—to try to help people who have not shared that unique experience to understand it, to imagine how it would feel. It's like this...

When you're going to have a baby, it's like planning a fabulous vacation trip—to Italy. You buy a bunch of guidebooks and make wonderful plans. The Colosseum. The Michelangelo *David.* The gondolas in Venice. You may learn some handy phrases in Italian. It's all very exciting.

After months of eager anticipation, the day finally arrives. You pack your bags and off you go. Several hours later, the plane lands. The stewardess comes in and says, "Welcome to Holland."

"Holland??!" you say. "What do you mean, Holland?? I signed up for Italy! I'm supposed to be in Italy. All my life I've dreamed of going to Italy."

But there's been a change in the flight plan. They've landed in Holland and there you must stay. The important thing is that they haven't taken you to a horrible, disgusting, filthy place, full of pestilence, famine and disease. It's just a different place.

So you must go out and buy new guidebooks. And you must learn a whole new language. And you will meet a whole new group of people you would never have met.

It's just a different place. It's slower paced than Italy, less flashy than Italy. But after you've been there for a while you catch your breath, you look around...and you begin to notice that Holland has windmills...and Holland has tulips. Holland even has Rembrandts.

But everyone you know is busy coming and going from Italy...and they're all bragging about what a wonderful time they had there. And for the rest of your life, you will say, "Yes, that's where I was supposed to go. That's what I had planned."

And the pain of that will never, ever, ever, ever go away.... Because the loss of that dream is a very, very significant loss.

But...if you spend your life mourning the fact that you didn't get to Italy, you may never be free to enjoy the very special, the very lovely things...about Holland.[4]

A Balanced Outlook

When retail tycoon J. C. Penney was asked the secret to his success, he replied, "Adversity. I would never have amounted to anything had I not been forced to come up the hard way." Of course, there is a balance. We don't want to *invite* pain into our children's lives! But when it does come, we must teach them how to handle it properly. A positive mom doesn't take away her children's troubles; she teaches them how to look for the hand of God in the midst of them. She teaches them how to think, react, and develop through the tough times.

If your son doesn't make a certain athletic team at school, what should you do? Allow him to grieve, then point him in the direction of a new sport or opportunity. If he makes a bad grade, use it as an opportunity to teach him a better way to study for the next test, or encourage him to ask the teacher for help. If your daughter's best friend moves away, allow her to cry, then provide opportunities for her to build new friendships. Remember, it is not the situation but the *reaction* to the situation that matters most.

I recently heard of a teenage girl who didn't make the cheerleading squad in high school. Her mother didn't want her to be sad, so she bought the girl a new car and let her miss a day of school so she could go to a local spa for a massage, a facial—the works. I couldn't help but wonder: What will this girl do in the future when she doesn't have her mother to buy away her sorrows? If she is never allowed to feel disappointment or pain, if she is never taught how to respond and grow through adversity, how will she get through life? Some people choose to avoid pain through drugs, alcohol, binge eating, shopping, sex, or some other escape.

As positive moms, let's give our children a balanced outlook on life. Yes, there is pain in this world. There is disappointment. There is struggle. But there is also God. And according to his Word, "he will never leave you nor forsake you" (Deuteronomy 31:6). He is working out "all things...for the good of those who love him" (Romans 8:28).

We can read countless stories in the Bible of people who experienced at least as many struggles as victories in their lives—from Adam to Noah to King David to John the Baptist. Even God's own Son suffered and died; yet without his willingness to experience tribulation, we would not have the forgiveness of our sins. Thank the Lord that he brings redemption from heartache and healing from sorrow!

If you are struggling with a situation in your life right now, don't be discouraged. Spiritual growth always comes through struggle. Allow God to use this circumstance to polish you, to perfect you, to complete the work he started in your life. Take encouragement from these words of Paul in 2 Corinthians 4:16–18: "Therefore we do not lose heart. Though outwardly we are wasting away, yet inwardly we are being renewed day by day. For our light and momentary troubles are achieving for us an eternal glory that far outweighs them all. So we fix our eyes not on what is seen, but on what is unseen. For what is seen is temporary, but what is unseen is eternal."

Ordered Steps

We never know when life will throw us a curve ball. Adversity can come upon us in an instant. But while we might be surprised by the turn of events, God never is.

Just ask my friend Leslie and her nine-year-old daughter, Amanda. This precious pair was driving to a special tea hosted by one of Amanda's friends on Valentine's Day 2000. With every mile, their anticipation and excitement rose. Finally they had only one more intersection ahead of them. But just as they were crossing the six lanes of traffic, a pickup truck rammed into the passenger side of the vehicle, flipping the car and landing it upside down. After the car came to rest, Leslie's maternal survival instinct took over. She managed to unbuckle her seat belt and carefully slide over to Amanda, who was still buckled in and hanging upside down. She released her daughter's seat belt, and together they crawled out through a shattered window and walked to safety. Leslie escaped with three cracked ribs and a partially collapsed lung; Amanda had a swollen right eye. It was a miracle that their injuries were not more serious!

Of course, Leslie and Amanda had not planned to spend the day in the emergency room, deal with a totaled automobile (it was a new car, by the way!), and devote the next few weeks to doctors' appointments and rehabilitation. But God allows certain unplanned adventures in our lives for reasons we may never know.

He also provides the help we need to make it through. At the time of the accident, a paramedic was on her way to work at a nearby hospital. She was the first one on the scene to help Leslie and Amanda through their ordeal. Then friends who were also on their way to the tea arrived one by one at the intersection. Within minutes, Amanda and Leslie were surrounded by medical help and supportive friends! As they will tell you, the hand of God was clearly covering them in the midst of their unexpected challenge.

Several days after the accident, Leslie discovered Psalm 37:23–24: "The steps of a good man are ordered by the LORD, and He delights in his way. Though he fall, he shall not be utterly cast down; for the LORD upholds him with His hand" (NKJV). Like Leslie, you and I have a wonderful heavenly Father who is watching over us, ordering our steps. He knows what we need to grow as strong, positive moms.

Yes, the winds will blow. The rains will come. The fires will burn. But God promises to be with us—"our refuge and strength, an ever-present help in trouble" (Psalm 46:1). He will give us all the grace we need to make it through.

POWER POINT

Read: The story of Ruth in the Bible (found in the Old Testament book of Ruth). List the difficulties she faced in her life, then write down the blessings God brought to her as well.

Pray: Oh Lord, my comfort and my strength, thank you for always being with me. Thank you for holding my hand. Thank you that although I may stumble, I will not fall, for you are there to hold me up. I trust that whatever happens to me and my family is filtered first through your loving hands. Strengthen me through the tough times. Help my children to grow through their own times of sadness, frustration, and disappointment. Help us to trust and honor you through all the circumstances and challenges in life.

Do: Make a "Life Map" to illustrate the significant events in your life—both the wonderful times and the difficult times. Set it up as a time line, and, if you want to get creative, include photos or illustrations. When you have finished, share your Life Map with your family. Talk about how God has brought something positive out of the good times and the bad times in your life.

Principle #4

THe Power of Strong Relationships

As iron sharpens iron, so one man sharpens another.
—Proverbs 27:17

Jesus made it clear that the most important thing in the world is our relationship to God and to others. When we achieve that, everything good will follow.
—Norman Vincent Peale

12

Harmony with Hubby
Keep Fanning the Flame

*It is the man and woman united that make the complete human
being. Separate, she wants his force of body and strength of reason;
he, her softness, sensibility and acute discernment. Together, they
are most likely to succeed in the world.*
—Benjamin Franklin

One winter several years ago we made a novel purchase: We
bought a fire pit. It's nothing spectacular, but it allows our little
suburban family living on the outskirts of Dallas to build a fire and
roast marshmallows in our own backyard. We love sitting and talking
around the fire while enjoying the rustic smell and the wonderful night
breeze.

We have found that the firelight works as a sort of truth serum.
People tend to relax, unwind, and share personal stories while sitting
together around a roaring blaze. But eventually the fire dies down. If we
want to keep the fire going—and extend that pleasant time of intimacy
and sharing—we have to get up, poke the ashes, and add a few more logs.

Marriages are like fires; they both need constant tending. We can't sit
back at any point and say, "There now, my marriage is fine. I don't have
to give to it anymore." This philosophy doesn't work for a campfire, and
it doesn't work for the home fire either. We must continue to be attentive
to our relationships with our husbands in order to keep the flames alive.

One of the cornerstones for building a strong family is a good marriage. Notice I did not say a *perfect* marriage. Everyone has his or her

imperfections. We must have realistic expectations as to what a marriage between two imperfect people ought to be.

At the same time, we must recognize that a positive husband-wife team has an invaluable impact on the family. Truly one of the best things we can do for our children is to pursue harmony with our hubbies, doing our part to strengthen our marriages. Of course, our husbands have their part too. It takes two to make a marriage. But as positive moms, we want to make sure we're doing everything we can to keep the marriage flame glowing and growing. Let's examine several logs we can put on the fire to keep our marriages strong.

Fire Builder #1: Love Your Husband

You wouldn't think we would need to be told to love our spouses. Didn't we commit to love them the day we married them? Even so, many marriages break up because spouses claim they just don't love their marriage partners anymore. They say they have fallen out of love—as if love is something a person can fall in and out of.

Since love is the key basis for our marriage commitment, we ought to have a better understanding of what it is. Think back. When you started dating the man who would become your spouse, you probably got those warm, fuzzy feelings that often come with the building of a new relationship. Those feelings were wonderful. They *are* wonderful. But ultimately, they cannot be the sole basis for love and commitment in marriage.

The roots of love run much deeper than just the surface foliage of sweet, romantic feelings and likable moments. Rather, love is a choice—a deliberate act of compassion based on our will, not just our emotions. It is not based necessarily on finding the right person (although marriage is one of the most important decisions in our lives and must be considered carefully and prayerfully). Rather, it is based on a commitment that we will continually accept the one to whom we've pledged our life, for better or worse.

True love is not easy. It requires devotion, forgiveness, loyalty, and selflessness. When we commit to marry someone, we make the choice to love that person through his weaknesses and strengths, his failures and successes. We make a decision to put down roots in our new life together.

We can even *learn* to love a person—whether or not we like him at that moment. We simply need to make the deliberate choice to love, then follow up that decision with action. If we truly love someone, what will we do for him? What actions will we take? Write him a note? Help him with a project? Cook his favorite meal? Give him a smile when he comes in the door?

In his book *The Five Languages of Love: How to Express Heartfelt Commitment to Your Mate*, author Gary Chapman describes the various ways different individuals give and receive love.[1] We're not all the same. What makes you feel loved might not be what will make your spouse feel loved. (In fact, you can probably count on it!) This evening, ask your husband what you can do to make him feel loved, and then begin to do the actions day by day. When you do the actions of love, the feelings will follow.

One of those all-important love-actions is forgiveness. God's love, of course, includes forgiveness. He forgives us even when we don't deserve it. In the same way, the Bible says, we are to forgive others: "Be kind and compassionate to one another, forgiving each other, just as in Christ God forgave you" (Ephesians 4:32). What are you holding over your spouse's head? Do you need to forgive him? Remember, God has forgiven you of all your faults; how can you withhold forgiveness from someone else?

As an imperfect wife, I am thankful for the forgiveness Curt has shown me through the years. The error in my checkbook, the dent in the car (and the damage to the fence by the driveway), the mess that

A successful marriage is an edifice that must be rebuilt every day. —Andre Maurois

occurred when I let the dog in with muddy feet—these situations (and many more) were opportunities for me to receive forgiveness when I really needed it. I appreciate that Curt forgives my shortcomings, and I try to extend that same forgiveness to him, recognizing that each one of us is imperfect in many ways. Who isn't?

Of course, in a physically abusive relationship or one riddled with infidelity, forgiveness does not mean allowing your spouse to continue his destructive behavior. You can forgive in your heart yet maintain boundaries and limits. True compassion and forgiveness mean helping your spouse stop his a destructive lifestyle by showing tough love. If you are in a situation like this, I recommend seeking wise counsel and reading the book *Love Must Be Tough: Proven Hope for Families in Crisis* by James Dobson.[2]

Fire Builder #2: Respect Him

What do men need most? Many husbands agree that respect is high on their list of needs. God already knew this, of course, and wrote it into his directions for marriage: "Each one of you [husbands] must love his wife as he loves himself, and the wife must respect her husband" (Ephesians 5:33).

Respecting one another is paramount in keeping a marriage strong and positive. Often the bottom line in a divorce is the wife's loss of respect for her partner. But what exactly is respect, and how do you show it?

To respect a spouse is to reverence, honor, and esteem him. When a wife does that, she finds that her husband lives up to the honor more often than not. In fact, husbands can go farther and higher in their God-given pursuits when they know that their wives believe in them and are backing them. As Proverbs 12:4 says, "A wife of noble character is her husband's crown." Make him feel like a king, and you'll be the queen reigning by his side!

But respect isn't always easy. In marriage, there may be times when our husbands disappoint us, bother us, or even disgust us. Consider Susan, who met her husband, Rick, in college where he was a star football player. As far as she was concerned, Rick hung the moon. But real life is different than the thrill of the university years, and now Rick just can't seem to find the right job. After years of jumping from business opportunity to business opportunity, they remain in debt to both parents and numerous credit-card companies. What once was a blissful dream has come to be a real-life nightmare. Susan has lost all respect for Rick. "He isn't a hard worker, he can't hold a job, and he certainly can't provide for his family!" she tells her friends.

Does Susan's story sound familiar? The details may be different, but many women find themselves in a relationship where respect has been lost. The sad thing about a wife who disrespects her husband is that she tends to see only what is wrong with her spouse. Her eyes, heart, and mind dwell only on the problems. She tends to forget two important truths: Although her husband has some glaringly bad qualities, he also has some good qualities (probably the ones for which she married him); and while it might seem impossible for her spouse to get his act together, "with God all things are possible" (Matthew 19:26).

Whenever we accentuate the positive qualities in other people, the negative qualities begin to dwindle. In Susan's case, she needs to remember that Rick is both a good family man and a spiritual leader in their home. If she could begin to focus on these positives, she could help her husband grow in confidence and overcome some of his weaknesses. Instead of verbally beating him up, she could praise him for what he does right and encourage him to find a job where his gifts and talents are best used. What a difference that change of focus would make in her home!

If you are struggling with a loss of respect for your husband, decide

A wife of noble character is her husband's crown, but a disgraceful wife is like decay in his bones. —Proverbs 12:4

☺

today that you will stop focusing on his bad qualities. Honor your husband when he is not around by guarding your tongue and not tearing him down in front of others. If you can't say anything nice about him, remember what you learned in kindergarten: Don't say anything at all.

Begin praying now, not only for your spouse, but for your response to him. Spend time each day thanking God for the good qualities in your husband and for the way God has made him. Pray that God would continue to develop your husband to grow according to God's plan for his life. Your husband needs your prayer support more than he needs your pressure or condemnation. Be patient and allow the Lord to work in his timing. Ask God to help you be a supportive wife, honoring and respecting your mate through the process.

On a daily basis, show your respect for your husband through your choice of words. Are you communicating respect in your message and your tone of voice? It can be so easy for us to speak our minds and lash out with our words; it is much harder to hold our tongues and treat our husbands with esteem! You can also show respect through such love-actions as:

- Sending a quick note to his office that says "I believe in you because..."
- Getting up early to fix him a good breakfast before the big presentation.
- Complimenting him in front of the kids and others.
- Listening to his point of view when he is up against a challenge.

Our children need to see our respect for our spouses. They need to know that we revere our husbands as the authority in the household who must answer to God for their leadership. What our kids see modeled by us will affect the kind of spouses they will grow up to be. It will also affect their view of God, since the marriage relationship is a picture of Christ and the church: "For the husband is the head of the wife as Christ is the head of the church.... Husbands, love your wives, just as Christ loved the church and gave himself up for her" (Ephesians 5:23, 25).

Fire Builder #3: Enjoy Him

Here's a log that is fun to throw on the fire: Enjoy your husband! Laugh together! Do fun things with each other! Enjoy your relationship! Life is too short to take it seriously 100 percent of the time. Unfortunately our busy schedules, career pressures, and family cares seem to keep our minds occupied to the point of eliminating any time for fun. You have to wonder: Is it possible in today's world to simply enjoy one another and create memorable moments outside of the normal routine? The answer is yes—but it takes a strong dose of both will power and creativity.

To get you started, here are a few ideas to help you add a little fun and flair to your marriage:

In the Home

Plan a romantic dinner. Now and then, put the kids to bed a little early and have a candlelight dinner. Prepare your husband's favorite meal, dim the lights, light the candles, and play his favorite CD.

Watch a video. After the kids are in bed, snuggle up on the couch and watch a movie together. Laugh together, cry together, enjoy one another.

Read a book. If you both enjoy reading, read a book together. Start a fire in the fireplace and turn on some soft background music to help you relax. If the kids are awake, encourage them to read or watch a video while you and Daddy read together.

Cook together. Pick a challenging recipe that you think both of you will enjoy. Split up the chopping, mixing, and sautéing duties and cook the meal together.

Have a romantic rendezvous. Prepare the environment with low lights, scented candles, and quiet music. Wear something fun and new. Be adventurous!

Outside the Home

Visit the local bookstore/coffee shop. Go together to a local coffee shop or bookstore (often these can be found under the same roof). Curt and I love to get a cup of coffee at our favorite bookstore around the corner and look at different books or sample new CDs together.

Make a date. What is something special and entertaining that you both like to do? Do you like to go to the movies, the ball game, the amusement park, the theater, the symphony? Save your money, make a date, and go out on a regular basis.

Do something for someone else. Serve dinner at a homeless shelter, help a friend move, visit a lonely relative. As you and your spouse join together to help someone else, your own bond grows stronger.

Take a trip. I know it is hard to leave the children, but every couple needs a little time to themselves. Even a short weekend away can help you focus on each other and learn to enjoy one another once again. If you don't have family in town to help you watch the kids, consider hiring a single person or a couple from your church or even one of your kids' schoolteachers.

Do something spontaneous. Although there are times when it's fun to plan ahead for a special event, last-minute surprises can be great too. Be spontaneous! Call a friend this afternoon and tell her you'll watch her kids one night if she'll watch yours tonight. Then surprise your husband with a special night out or a romantic evening at home.

Make a tradition. Choose a holiday tradition that only you and your husband will do together—without the kids. After the children are grown, you will have many holidays when it is just the two of you.

Establish a fun tradition now that you will enjoy every year for the rest of your life together.

Exercise together. Choose a sport or activity that you both enjoy and start working out together. Since our daughters are old enough to be home alone, Curt and I enjoy taking evening walks—just the two of us. These have become our special times to talk, discuss the issues we're facing, or share the joys of our day. Our walks are reminiscent of our dating relationship in college, when we would run together and train for distance races. Now, in deference to our aging knee joints, we walk instead of run—but we enjoy the pleasure of being exercise companions once again.

The Essential Ingredient

Of all the ingredients necessary to keep a fire burning, one ingredient is invisible but absolutely essential: oxygen. In our marriages, that critical but invisible ingredient is God. Even Christian couples are often guilty of not making the Lord an essential part of their marriage. But it is God's example of love that encourages us to love. It is his example of forgiveness that prompts us to forgive. It is his Spirit within us that helps us to love in a way that often surpasses human ability or understanding. Hebrews 12:29 describes God as "a consuming fire," and it is his flame that can ignite the barely glowing embers of struggling marriages, renewing the fire of love we have for our mates.

How do we bring God into our marriages? One of the best ways is to pray with our spouses on a regular basis. From the first day of our marriage, Curt and I began to form the habit of praying together each night before going to sleep. Eighteen years later, we are still praying. Those nightly prayer times remind us of the source of our strength and help, and turn our eyes together toward God's faithfulness and love.

Some husbands and wives read the Scriptures together; others attend a couples' Bible study at their church. However you choose to draw closer together spiritually, the important thing is that you and your husband make your relationship with God the central element of your marriage. Through the difficulties as well as in the blessed times, turn to God together for strength and direction. He is your all in all, in marriage as in all of life. May his undying love be the glue that seals your hearts together!

POWER POINT

Read: The entire book of Song of Solomon. Notice the love, respect, and enjoyment this couple has for one another.

Pray: O wonderful Father in heaven, I praise you, for you are love. You love me so perfectly and completely! Thank you. Fill me with your loving-kindness and forgiveness, especially toward my husband. Help me to love my husband as you love me. Help me to respect my spouse, honoring him and holding him in high esteem. Help me to overlook his faults and focus on his strengths. Help me to be an encourager. Give me the will power and the creativity to keep the flame strong in our marriage. Please bless and keep our marriage so we may glorify you in our union, knowing we are a picture of Christ and the church. Thank you for putting such a high value on marriage, and may we magnify you together! In Jesus' name, amen.

Do: Choose one of the ideas in this chapter for enjoying your spouse. Set a date, make plans, and carry them through!

Affirming Friendships
The Value of a Wise Companion

If a man does not make new acquaintances as he advances through life, he will soon find himself left alone; one should keep his friendships in constant repair.
—Samuel Johnson

Connie and Sandra enjoy meeting at the park or the local McDonald's at least once a week. It is a ritual they formed over the years, since the time their children were toddlers. As the kids play, the two moms talk about every topic under the sun, from preschools to potty training. Frequently during the week they help each other out by watching each other's children, running errands, and sharing information about a hot sale at the grocery store. Most importantly, they care for one another and offer a shoulder to cry on when one has a child who is struggling or the other has a husband who "just doesn't understand." One can hardly put a price on a friendship such as Connie and Sandra's!

Sadly our busy lives, overloaded with the responsibilities of modern motherhood, tend to make it difficult to develop and deepen new and abiding relationships. Many moms today wonder: Is it possible to develop lifelong, heart-to-heart friendships in such a "hurry-up, rush-around" world?

Let's consider for a moment how a relationship develops. Most of us have many acquaintances in our everyday lives. If we were to count, the number might run in the dozens, or even the hundreds. These are people we know, but not well. They go to church with us; their children go to school with our children; they're at the same Little League games; they shop at the same stores we do; they work in the same building as we do. We may know their names; we may not. But we run into them with some regularity due to the places we go and the activities we participate in each week.

An acquaintance is someone with whom we carry on the typical surface conversation. You know the lingo:

"Hello, how are you?"
"Fine, how are you?"
"Fine."
"Glad to hear it. Well, talk to you later."
"Okay, 'bye."
" 'Bye."

Sometimes we may step out of the normal boundaries and talk about the weather or how cute the kids were in the musical, but generally we keep the conversation quite safe and shallow. Every once in a while, however, we find someone from this pool of acquaintances with whom we seem to connect on a deeper level. We find a potential friend.

Friendship tends to happen out of the blue. In one of those "aha!" moments, we realize that the other person shares a connection with us, whether it is a common viewpoint, a similar idea, or children with the same interests—and a companionship is born. The word *companion* means someone who walks with us in the same direction; it denotes someone with whom we can relate and with whom we can begin to build trust. Even Jesus needed companionship in his life on earth, and the four Gospels tell how he drew twelve companions from among his large pool of acquaintances and followers.

If we make that connection into companionship with someone we've known on the acquaintance level, then eventually, through nurturing and growth, that relationship has the potential to grow into a deep and lasting friendship. We might say we have a "soul mate." We can count ourselves fortunate if we develop two or three soul mates in a lifetime. A true heart-friend of this nature is one with whom we can share our lives on a deep level, revealing our hopes and fears, disappointments and dreams. Such friends love us unconditionally and understand us without having to say a word. They are with us for the long haul. Even when we're separated from a soul mate for months or even years, we can always pick right up where we left off without skipping a beat.

Of course, your husband should fit into the soul-mate category of your life. If he doesn't, you need to reread the previous chapter! But for now, I want us to focus mainly on friends outside of our family circles. Jesus had three especially close friends: Peter, James, and John. These friends, drawn from his larger circle of twelve companions, accompanied Christ to the Mount of Transfiguration and saw him revealed in all his glory. They were the ones he asked to stay nearby while he travailed in prayer in the Garden of Gethsemane.

Close friendships like these are much like a garden of beautiful flowers. Just as flowers need water, sunshine, and the proper nutrients in order to bloom and grow, friendships need love, care, and attention to develop and deepen. What can we do to nurture our lovely garden of growing relationships? Let's look at three keys:

Key #1: Make Friendship a Priority

In his book *The Friendship Factor*, Alan Loy McGinnis states that the main reason people do not experience deep and abiding relationships is because they do not make them a priority in their lives.[1] How important are friendships to you? As a busy mother, you certainly have a few other things to think about! Your husband and kids need you first, of course. Next you are probably focused on work or volunteer duties at the school, the church, and in the community. Friendships may fall dead last in your order of priorities!

As we consider the priorities in our lives, it is always good to reflect on God's priorities. Clearly relationships are important in the Bible. Think back to the Garden of Eden and the Creation account in Genesis 1 and 2. After God finished creating the whole world, he saw that everything was good—that is, *almost* everything. "It is not good for the man to be alone," God said in Genesis 2:18. Adam had everything he could possibly want. He was living in paradise, walking in a wonderful relationship with his creator. Still, something was missing. He needed a companion, someone with whom he could relate.

We know that God created Eve at that point to be Adam's helpmate. But other friendships are also important to both men and women. Wise King Solomon recognized the importance of friends when he said, "As iron sharpens iron, so one man sharpens another" (Proverbs 27:17). The friends God puts in our lives challenge us and sharpen us, helping us become better people. Do you have a knife drawer in your kitchen? I do, but I tend to use only about half of the knives in the drawer. Why? Because the other half have grown dull, and I have not taken the time to get the blades sharpened. They just sit in the drawer, not useful for anything. Without friends, we can become like those dull knives; but through good friendships, we are continuously sharpened and made useful in God's kingdom.

While not talking about friendships specifically, Jesus explained how important it was to love others when he was asked, "Teacher, which is the greatest commandment in the Law?" (Matthew 22:36). Jesus answered, "Love the Lord your God with all your heart and with

And let us consider how we may spur one another on toward love and good deeds. —Hebrew 10:24

all your soul and with all your mind. This is the first and greatest commandment. And the second is like it: Love your neighbor as yourself" (vv. 37–39). According to Jesus, second only to relating well to God is the importance of relating well to other people!

Jesus lived this love for others in his own life. Clearly, he devoted himself to his friends. We only need to read his prayer for his disciples in John 17:6–19 to see how much he loved them! Following in the Lord's footsteps, the apostle Paul also gave priority to relationships: "Be devoted to one another in brotherly love. Honor one another above yourselves," he wrote in Romans 12:10.

I believe that mothers especially need one another as friends. We need the companionship, the camaraderie, and the understanding that another woman can give. We need to help each other. Sometimes we need to be picked up and pointed in a positive direction, and an affirming friend can be just the one to do that. Truly a friend is a gift from God, given to us to share our joys as well as to help us get through life's challenges.

So how do we make friendships a priority in the midst of our admittedly crowded lives? By first recognizing those friendships that are important to us and then being a good friend. As Emerson said, "The only way to have a friend is to be one."[2]

To maintain the friendships that are important to me, I've made it a point to set aside certain times during the month to get together. I have one friend with whom I keep a standing lunch date on the second Tuesday of every month. With another friend, I get together on a weekly basis to pray. I meet with two other friends (we make a delightful threesome!) every other Thursday to chat, laugh, and pray. One of my dearest friends and I talk on the phone several times a week and get together for lunch when we can. I've found it helpful to put regular meetings with my friends on the calendar so that the "tyranny of the urgent" doesn't cause me to miss out on the relationships I hold dear.

Being a friend doesn't necessarily have to take a lot of time; it just takes a little kindness, a little thoughtfulness, a little compassion toward others—and a little planning. It also takes obedience to the Word of God. As we begin to live out the principles of Christian love found in Scripture, we will begin to find ourselves becoming better friends to one another.

Key #2: Build on a Common Interest

Put any two mothers next to each other in a doctor's waiting room, and within minutes they can be deep in conversation on any of a number of topics ranging from childhood diseases to favorite children's books. As mothers, we have a basic camaraderie born out of similar experience. And as we learn to build on these common interests, we can begin to see strong relationships blossom.

The good news is that building a friendship doesn't necessarily take time away from family responsibilities. In fact, a good friendship can grow even while we keep our husbands and children a priority. Want to take the kids to the park for the afternoon? Call an acquaintance with kids the same age as yours and ask them to join you. The children will grow in their social skills as they play with one another, and you will have the opportunity to develop a friendship yourself. Need to go to the farmers market or a wholesale store? Invite a friend to go with you and split the bulk-quantity items. Taking the kids to the newest G-rated movie in town? Don't go alone. Invite an acquaintance and her children and build a budding friendship as you all experience the silver screen together. Then go for ice cream or hot chocolate afterward.

Organize a playgroup with acquaintances who have kids the same age as yours. Or join one of the many wonderful mothers organizations in your area, such as MOPS (Mothers of Preschoolers), Early Childhood PTA, Preschool PTA, or Moms Club. (Check for listings in the newspaper or a local parent publication for groups in your area.) Many churches have regular moms' groups as well. If you can't find one, maybe you can start one! Friendships are just waiting to be born and developed from these wonderful circles of shared experiences.

Of course, I'm not suggesting that we spend all of our time in mothers groups or that we call a friend every time we go somewhere. We do need time alone with our families. But we should try to take advantage of friend-making opportunities when it is appropriate. Just be balanced! We don't want to grow dependent upon having company in everything we do, and we don't want our kids to think that we must have someone with us every second. But while we all need some guarded family time, we also need some blessed friendship time. Our kids need to see us making the effort to reach out to others in friendship. They'll learn to do the same by watching our example.

In chapter 8, we talked about the blessing of finding a prayer partner. Certainly, one of the deepest bonds we can have with a friend is the bond that forms when we pray together. Four years ago, my friend Carol and I began to realize that we had a common devotion to prayer for our families. We decided that we should try to meet together once a week to pray for the specific needs of our four daughters. (Each of us has two girls.) The depth of our friendship continues to deepen because of those precious prayer times. Today Carol and I can share anything with each other. We have an abiding trust and love that has been built over the years on our common interest in prayer.

Have you found something in common with an acquaintance? Similar hobbies, kids the same age, a common enthusiasm for sports? Do you love to shop at the same stores? Read the same books? Whatever your common interest, build on it! You will find a natural relationship beginning to form. Then, as trust develops over time, you will find yourself sharing at ever-deepening levels of honesty and openness. One word of caution: Make sure you know your friend is a loyal person before you begin to really open up. Few things hurt more than having a confidence betrayed by someone you thought you could trust. But once trust is built, be open, honest, and real—and enjoy the blessing of your God-given friendship.

Key #3: Encourage One Another

Beth is a positive friend. Whenever I am down, whenever I feel as though I have messed up as a mother, Beth is there to give me a good word and assure me that everything will be okay. She points me to God and to Scripture. Sometimes I am asked to talk about my books on local radio talk shows, and after I've gone off the air I can depend on Beth to call me up afterward and say, "You were great! I'm proud you're my friend!"

Beth is one of those rare treasures: a true encourager. She never engages in putting people down. She takes no pleasure in watching someone's demise. She always tries to see the good in every situation. If I have a disagreement with my husband and begin to complain, she tells me how lucky I am to have Curt and reminds me of his finer qualities (which far outweigh his negatives).

I am definitely a better person because of Beth! Everyone needs an affirming friend just like her. People who grumble and complain are a dime a dozen, but a friend who gives strength through encouragement is worth her weight in gold.

A number of years ago, I had a friend who was the exact opposite of Beth. She put down everything in my life, including my husband. "Oh, he just doesn't understand you," she'd say. "I'll pray for him—he needs it!" She put down everything and everyone in my life, from my children's school to people in our Bible study.

Surely we contend with enough negative influences in our world today without being bombarded by them in our friendships! I eventually recognized that I needed to discontinue this relationship because I was beginning to be influenced in a negative way toward my family. Instead of helping me see the blessings in my life, this friend was leading me to focus on the few things that were wrong.

Remember the story of the Israelites grumbling in the wilderness? God miraculously arranged their escape from slavery in Egypt and took care of their every need. He gave them a great leader in Moses. Yet they lost their focus on what God was going to do in and through them and worked themselves into believing that life would be better if they were back in Egypt as slaves! How do you think they became such complainers? It probably started with a few grumblers, who spread their negative thoughts to others, who complained to still others, and before they knew it, discouragement had seeped into the hearts of almost everyone. Poor Moses! At least he had two positive friends, Caleb and Joshua, who didn't focus on what was wrong with the situation but focused on what God could do in the midst of it.

What kind of friends do you have? Are they Calebs and Joshuas, or are they grumblers and complainers? Remember, positive friendships make a difference in your life, but so do negative ones. I know of a number of situations in which negative friendships have led to frustration, discontentment, and even divorce. Are your friendships making you better, or bitter? Pray that God will lead you to women who can help you see things from a godly perspective and not a self-centered, earthly one. Surround yourself with friends who are uplifters and not downtrodders—and remember to be that positive influence in your friends' lives in return.

Friendships with other women make our lives incredibly rich. You and I don't need a lot of money to be wealthy. We just need a few good friends!

A friend loves at all times. —Proverbs 17:17

POWER POINT

Read: 1 Samuel 20. Notice that Jonathan and David had a profound and positive friendship, despite many obstacles. Also read Colossians 3:1–17, which provides a wonderful picture of the qualities of a positive friend.

Pray: Most holy and wonderful Lord, you are the perfect friend. You are always there for me. You meet my every need. Thank you for the friends you have brought into my life. Help me to be attentive to these friendships. Help me to be a better friend. Help me to see the new, potential friends you put in my path each day. In Jesus' name, amen.

Do: In a notebook or prayer journal, make three lists: Acquaintances, Companions, and Soul Mates. Fill it in with names of people who are currently in your life. Pray about working to deepen some of these relationships. Pray for each friend by name.

Mentor Moms
Building Relationships with Seasoned Mothers

*As she supplies the affection and care that make a contented home,
each mother is strengthening the individuals within her
own circle as well as in the nation.*
—Earl E. Chanley

As the Director of Women's Ministries at a large Bible church in Dallas, Vickie Kraft wanted to find a way to draw out the gifts that God had given to each of the women in her congregation. She also wanted to meet their various needs as best she could. Eventually she found a way to do both at the same time. The more mature women, she realized, possessed wisdom and experience that could be shared with the younger women. Using Paul's instructions in Titus 2:3–4 as her basis—"the older women…can train the younger women"—she organized a program that she called Heart to Heart, pairing mature women with younger women in mentoring relationships.

After Vickie was interviewed on the popular *Focus on the Family* radio program with Dr. James Dobson, the Heart to Heart ministry quickly spread to congregations worldwide. Today Vickie is the author of several books on mentoring and speaks to women's groups across the nation and around the world, teaching them how to connect women to women in this dynamic program.

Why did Vickie's idea spread like wildfire? Clearly, it has a sound biblical basis, and God has given younger women—especially young mothers—a great desire for wise and seasoned mentors in their lives. Many young mothers in today's society don't have the benefit of living in the same community with the elder women in their families. Mothers, grandmothers, and other matriarchal figures are spread all over the globe, and younger women often must forge new territory on their own.

Meanwhile many older women have a desire to give of themselves and make an impact on the younger generation. Their own children are grown and often live far away. Still, they know that they have wisdom and gifts to share, and they often jump at the opportunity to share them with the younger women that come into their lives.

A mentoring relationship doesn't take the place of peers. Friendship with other women our own age and at the same level of experience is special; as we go through similar life experiences, we enjoy a wonderful camaraderie. But a relationship with a "mentor mom" is special too. Not only do we find caring companionship in a mentor, but we benefit from the wisdom and counsel of someone who's "been there." As we learn from our mentor's experience, we gain a more balanced perspective on life. What a relief it can be to hear such words of assurance as "Don't worry; it's just a phase" or "This too shall pass" or "Honey, I felt the same way when I was your age."

Nor can a mentor replace our own mothers or other family matriarchs. Still, a seasoned mother-friend can give advice to a new mother in ways that a family member sometimes cannot. Many times we don't receive advice well from people in our own families because of emotional ties or baggage from the past. In such cases, a wise woman speaking from outside the family circle can be a breath of fresh air!

Making the Connection

Whether there is a Heart to Heart ministry in your area or not, you can still begin to follow Paul's direction and seek to connect your life with a more seasoned mother. But how do you find the right mentor mom? Certainly you cannot force someone to be your mentor, but there are ways to easily and naturally grow into a mentoring relationship. Let's look at three steps that can lead to that special bond:

1. Pray

Begin now to pray that God would prepare the heart of a mature woman to be your mentor mom. Ask him to match you with someone who can encourage your strengths and help you grow through your weaknesses.

2. Inquire

Inquire at your church about women who may have an interest in being mentors. You may want to ask the leader in an older adult Sunday school class, or check with the person in charge of the women's ministry. Tell them you would like to connect with a spiritually mature, older mother who has the desire to influence or guide a younger mother.

3. Initiate

Don't wait for someone to come to you. Many times an older woman will feel awkward offering herself as a mentor; she may feel this implies that she has it all together. Once you discover a person with whom you feel you could connect, ask her to pray and consider being your mentor mom. Assure her that she doesn't need to be perfect, just willing to lend an ear, give some advice, and be a friend.

Of course, while you can't expect perfection in a mentor, you should look for certain qualities. The Bible tells us important attributes that a woman who leads or teaches others should have. In Titus 2:3 Paul writes, "Likewise, teach the older women to be reverent in the way they live, not to be slanderers or addicted to much wine, but to teach what is good." From this description we can see that a good mentor is a woman who lives a godly life. She is neither a heavy drinker nor a gossip, but one who lives and teaches biblical principles. Apparently Paul recognized that women whose families have left the nest can be tempted to idle away their time in gossip or selfish pursuits. His command is that older women use their time in a far more worthy way, by teaching younger women how to live for the Lord. When you identify a potential mentor, ask yourself: Does this person display a godly character and lifestyle? Your intent is to follow the instruction in Titus 2; make sure hers is too.

Building a Bond

Once you have established an association with your mentor mom, how do you begin forming a relationship and create closeness? Initially you simply need to make an effort to get to know each other. Ask your new friend to tell you about her children. Are they grown? Do they live in the area? Does she have grandchildren? Find out about her childhood and what life was like growing up in her family. Ask her how she met her husband. How did she become a Christian? Tell her about your life too. Share more than just the facts; allow her to see your feelings and emotions. As you open up with each other, you will begin to form a trust and an understanding between you.

Once you feel comfortable with one another, what do you do next? Titus 2:4–5 holds the key: "[The older women] can train the younger women to love their husbands and children, to be self-controlled and pure, to be busy at home, to be kind and to be subject to their husbands, so that no one will malign the word of God." Basically, mentor moms are called to impact the lives of young mothers by imparting spiritual encouragement and practical advice born of experience. This can be done informally by talking and spending time together, or more formally by going through a particular Bible study together. Many study guides are available to help. Perhaps a trip to the local Christian bookstore with your mentor can help you find the perfect study to interest you both.

Most importantly, you and your mentor mom can begin to pray with one another and for one another. Women with grown families often have more time to spend in faithful and diligent prayer. How wonderful to share your prayer requests with someone you know will take the time to pray! Remember to keep a journal of your prayer requests, and don't forget to record how God answers them in his perfect timing.

Planning Your Time

As mothers, we have many wonderful opportunities available to us; but if we do not guard our time, we will end up spending too much time away from our top priority, our family. Since time is precious and limited, it is important to consider the amount of time you want to spend with your mentor. I recommend beginning by meeting just once a month, with a set starting and stopping time. Having clear boundaries will help you and your mentor feel more comfortable about getting together again. If, after several months, you can both see your way clear to meet more than once a month, you might agree to spend some additional time together. Many times meeting once a month in person and talking once a month on the phone can be a good mix.

It helps to set a specific meeting day—say, the second Tuesday of every month. This helps you stay consistent; you won't be likely to schedule a dentist appointment on that day by mistake. Your telephone conversation can be scheduled the same way. Perhaps there is a time during the day when the kids are taking a nap or watching a favorite show, giving you a window of opportunity to have an uninterrupted phone conversation. Again, set a time limit. Twenty minutes is plenty of time to update one another and share prayer requests.

Where should you meet? A local park makes a good meeting place, weather permitting. This allows the kids to get exercise and fresh air while you keep watch over them and visit with your mentor. After my mother passed away, one of her good friends met my children and me regularly at the park for picnics and conversation. It was a delightful place to make memories together!

If the kids are at school or can be dropped off at a friend's house, you can meet your mentor at a restaurant over lunch. Visiting over a good meal is always fun, although a restaurant setting does lack the privacy you may want if you are doing a Bible study together. And, of course, you can always meet at your home so you can chat while the baby is napping or the kids are playing nearby.

Throughout the seasons of my life, God has brought several mentor moms into my life. With some, I met regularly and deliberately; with others, I met just a few times or on a sporadic basis. But each woman made a strong impact on my life. Barbara was there for me just after my mother passed away. Norma encouraged me during the challenging years of raising preschoolers. Anne was a godly prayer warrior who helped me during the formative years of my speaking and writing ministry. Jan, Donna, and Doris were (and still are) great blessings to my family and me. My life has been made richer through my relationships with these wonderful mentors.

On the Other Side

I always considered myself to be the one on the younger side of the mentor couplet. But at some point, unbeknownst to me, I became qualified for the more mature side. Amazing how it happened so

Likewise, teach the older women to be reverent in the way they live.... Then they can train the younger women. —Titus 2:3–4

quickly! Now it's my turn to pour into a younger mother some of the wisdom and experience I've gained over the years. And I love it! As the saying goes, "When you hold a torch to light another's path, you brighten your own." What a blessing it is to walk alongside the younger women God brings into my life, helping them to love their husbands, care for their kids, and build their homes!

As mentors (yes, if you aren't there already, you will be), we can allow God to work through us, not only to teach and encourage others, but also to serve. If time allows, we can offer to help a younger friend by watching her children while she runs errands or cooking dinner for her family when she's sick in bed. We can send cards or write notes of encouragement, helping her smile when she feels tired or overwhelmed. We can stay on the lookout for ways to assist her as she raises her family to love and serve the Lord.

Perhaps you are not mature in years, but you are mature in the faith and have grown through the experiences and circumstances God has brought into your life. Age is not the sole qualifier for being a mentor. You, too, have much to share with women who are younger in their walk with God. We should always be ready to share whatever God has given us with the women he sends our way.

I want to close this chapter by telling you about Kaye and Lydia. These two women taught the two-year-olds' Sunday school class together at their church. Kaye was a young, single woman; Lydia was married with two preteen daughters. They became fast friends, despite the difference in their ages. When Lydia's daughters went through the assorted challenges of the preteen years, Kaye was able to offer a "big sister" kind of help. When Kaye met Robert at the singles ministry, Lydia was there to encourage her in the new relationship. Later Lydia helped Kaye make wedding plans. Now Kaye has preteen daughters of her own, and guess who she goes to for counsel and advice?

These two women are a blessing to each other because they were willing, years ago, to reach out and build a bond. Their special mentoring relationship continues to have a positive impact on both of their lives to this day. May we all be as blessed as Kaye and Lydia!

POWER POINT

Read: Colossians 3. How can this passage be applied to a mentoring relationship?

Pray: Wonderful Father, thank you for the privilege of being a mother. Thank you for the help you give me along the way. Thank you for the seasoned mothers you've brought into my life to help me and encourage me to honor you in my home. Lead me to mentors who can share their wisdom and experience with me. Open up opportunities to build friendships. Show me when it is my turn to mentor others and help me to be a godly example to those around me. In Jesus' name, amen.

Do: If you are a young mother, begin praying that God would lead you to a mature woman with whom you can connect in a mentoring relationship. Actively inquire about women in your church who may be willing to build a relationship. If you are a mature mother, ask God to give you opportunities to minister to others.

Principle #5

THe Power OF Your Example

*In the same way, let your light shine before men, that they may see
your good deeds and praise your Father in heaven.*
—Matthew 5:16

The first great gift we can bestow on others is a good example.
—Morell

15

Living Lesson Books
Your Actions Speak Louder Than Words

The foundations of character are built not by lecture,
but by bricks of good example, laid day by day.
—Leo B. Blessing

The Never Ending Story is a children's movie about a young boy named Bastian who loved to read. One day Bastian wandered into an antique bookstore and discovered a very odd storybook. He took it home, and, as he began to read, he found that he had entered the story and become part of the drama! He experienced incredible adventures in his quest to save the book's heroine, a beautiful, young princess. In the process, he grew in courage and bravery.

Near the end of the movie, Bastian's father began searching for him but could not find him. Finally the father picked up the old storybook and began to scan the pages. To his great astonishment, he found that he was reading about his own son! As the final chapter unfolded, the princess was restored to her throne, and Bastian returned from the pages of the book into his father's arms. Everyone, of course, lived happily ever after.[1]

Wouldn't it be incredible to actually jump into the pages of a book and live out the adventure in the text? In a way, our lives do represent the pages in a book. The title of the book is *Life's Living Lessons*. Our children read this book every day; they see our actions on the pages. It is possibly the most influential book they will ever read, with the exception of the Bible. In fact, reading it is guaranteed to be life changing!

What are some of the chapters in our *Living Lessons* saga? Hopefully, the Table of Contents reads something like this:

Chapter One: Maintaining Self-Control Even When You're Tired and Frustrated

Chapter Two: Showing Patience in Traffic Jams and Grocery Store Lines

Chapter Three: Saying Kind Things about Others

Chapter Four: Telling the Truth, Even about the Little Things

Chapter Five: Helping Others When They Need a Hand

Chapter Six: Grumbling Less, Complimenting More

Chapter Seven: Using Table Manners and Other Forms of Good Etiquette

Chapter Eight: Obeying Traffic Rules and Laws

Chapter Nine: Praying about All Things, Worrying about Nothing

Unfortunately, many of our texts read a little differently. Can you relate to the following chapter titles?

Chapter One: Losing My Temper in a Frazzled Moment in Time

Chapter Two: Frustration and Anger in the Checkout Line

Chapter Three: Telling Juicy Stories about Friends and Foes

Chapter Four: A Few White Lies Go a Long Way

Chapter Five: No Time to Care, I Have Enough Challenges of My Own

Chapter Six: Grumbling without Regret

Chapter Seven: Good Manners out the Window

Chapter Eight: Traffic Rules Were Made to Be Broken

Chapter Nine: Worry Now, Pray Later

Like it or not, our life is an open book, continually read by the little eyes in our homes. The lessons we deliver to our children verbally may be wise and good, but lasting lessons are caught, not taught. It is rather sobering to realize that all the "right stuff" that comes out of our mouths can be made null and void if our kids do not see good character qualities lived out in our day-to-day lives. An old Chinese proverb says, "Not the cry, but the flight of the wild duck, leads the flock to fly and follow." Where are we leading our little flock by our example? How can we become better living lesson books for our children?

Heaven Help Us

It's hard to be a good example. In fact, at times it seems downright impossible. The apostle Paul spoke about this common struggle of knowing what we should do, yet doing what we know we shouldn't. In Romans 7:18–25 he admitted, "For I have the desire to do what is good, but I cannot carry it out. For what I do is not the good I want to do; no, the evil I do not want to do—this I keep on doing. Now if I do what I do not want to do, it is no longer I who do it, but it is sin living in me that does it.... What a wretched man I am! Who will rescue me from this body of death? Thanks be to God—through Jesus Christ our Lord!"

Paul knew that apart from Christ, we are hopeless. But with Christ, all things are possible. Jesus gave his followers hope when he said, "I am the vine; you are the branches. If a man remains in me and I in him, he will bear much fruit; apart from me you can do nothing" (John 15:5). Trying to be a good example in our own power leads to eventual failure, but abiding in Christ brings fruitfulness and hope.

The analogy of the vine and the branches is a beautiful picture of Christ and his followers. Is it the branch's job to create the fruit and make it grow? No, the branch simply stays attached to the vine and receives the nourishment the vine brings. Detached from the vine, the branch cannot bear fruit. But as it stays connected to the vine day by day, the fruit begins to grow naturally.

How can you live as a good example in your home? Stay attached to the vine! Abide in Christ. Continue in him; keep following him; remain in him. Stay close. Live with him, just as a homeowner might say to a new tenant, "Come into my house and abide here."

Is Christ dwelling in you? Is he just an acquaintance, or is he an important part of your day to day life? Remember, without him you can do nothing!

Examples Speak Loud and Clear

There once were two mothers who lived next-door to one another. Both had children the same age, and both were, at the same moment, looking at the mess in their playrooms. The first mother called her children together and, getting down on her hands and knees, began demonstrating how to tidy up the room. Her children followed her lead, and they all finished cleaning up together. The second mother scolded her children, demanding that they get right to work and "do their part" to keep the house clean. With scowling faces and lead feet, the children put a few books back on the shelf then pushed the rest of the toys under the sofa.

The first mother showed by her example how to get the job done; the second used her mouth but not her hands. As you can imagine, the first mother made a positive impact on her children because she led by selfless example; the second mother simply engendered a growing bitterness in her children. Both mothers, whether they realized it or not, were teaching much more than just how to clean a playroom.

Taking the time to show our children how to do certain tasks speaks volumes to them. It says, "My mother cares enough to show me how it is done." Certainly it is much easier to tell a son that he needs to clean the windows or a daughter that she must mop the kitchen floor. But they will learn how to do it right if we take the time to demonstrate. Being an example not only takes character; it takes time. In our busy society, time is a precious commodity—which makes it even more valuable when we hand it to our children and say, "Here, honey, let me show you how to do that." From demonstrating the backstroke to teaching our children how to pray, our example lights the pathway to our children's own accomplishments.

We are all familiar with the old adage, "Give a man a fish, and he has food for a day. Teach a man how to fish and you have fed him for life." The story is told of a time when Saint Francis of Assisi asked a young monk to accompany him on a trip to a small village in order to preach the gospel. The monk was honored to be invited by such a great master and readily accepted the invitation. The two men spent the day walking the streets, byways, and alleys of the village, caring for the needs of the helpless and poor they met along the way. They ministered to hundreds of people in that one day. As nightfall approached, the two headed back home, and the young monk realized that Francis had not once gathered the crowds to preach the gospel message. Disappointed, he said, "I thought we were going to preach the gospel today." The master replied profoundly, "We did preach. We were preaching while we were walking. We were watched by many, and our behavior was closely observed. It is of no use to walk anywhere to preach unless we preach everywhere as we walk!"[2]

As a young girl, I often took walks with my grandfather in his hometown of Pekin, Illinois. Pekin is a small town with very little traffic; yet whenever we crossed a street, Grandpa would reach down and gently take my hand without saying a word. I got the message. It couldn't have been more loud and clear: "I love you. You are precious to

Set an example for the believers in speech, in life, in love, in faith and in purity. —1 Timothy 4:12

me, and I don't want anything to happen to you." I miss those walks with Grandpa. But now, every time I take a walk with my daughters in our little neighborhood, I reach down and take their hands when we cross a street. Call it a habit; I call it a message of love that I learned from my grandfather's example.

Nobody's Perfect

Bil Keane's "The Family Circus" is one of my favorite comic strips. One segment in particular illustrates the powerful influence our example plays in the lives of our children. The first of two frames shows little Jeffy riding his tricycle around the house shouting, "Move over!" "Stoopid!" "Make up yer mind!" The next frame shows his mother, wearing a concerned expression, asking Jeffy what he is doing. The little boy's proud reply: "Drivin' like Daddy!"[3] What would your children do if they imitated your actions on the road, at the checkout counter, in the kitchen after a long day? Stop and think for a moment. A little scary, isn't it? Now ask yourself: What kind of example would you like your children to be imitating?

In my own home, I'm beginning to see more and more of my reflection as I look at my teenage daughters. Thankfully I see some good traits; but I also see some of my negative traits popping up from time to time. It is a highly convicting moment when I hear my own child using the exact same whining words of complaint that I used in my last gripe session with Curt!

Of course, nobody's perfect. We have all done things that we regret. I think of Peter who denied that he even knew Jesus—not once, not twice, but three times. No doubt Peter felt like a total failure. How could God possibly use Peter to build the church when he displayed such obvious weakness? Peter learned—as we should—that God is a forgiving God. He "redeems [our] life from the pit and crowns [us] with love and compassion" (Psalm 103:4). He forgives us, renews us, and still uses us, despite our mistakes.

After Jesus was resurrected, he came to Peter and asked three times, "Peter, do you love me?" (Perhaps he asked the question three times as a balance to the three times the disciple had denied him.) Peter answered, "Lord, you know all things; you know that I love you." And Jesus told him, "Feed my sheep" (John 21:17). Peter had messed up, but God still had a great plan for Peter's life! Peter would become the leader of the first century church, feeding the precious followers who would soon come to know Christ as their Savior.

We, too, are bound to mess up from time to time. But thank the Lord, "If we confess our sins, he is faithful and just and will forgive us our sins and purify us from all unrighteousness" (1 John 1:9). God forgives us, and he can still use us! In fact, when we make a mistake, God can use us to teach our children by example how to humbly come before him, repent, and accept his wonderful mercy and love.

Our lives can be the best sermon our children ever hear. I love how this poem, attributed to Edgar Guest, puts it:

I'd rather see a sermon, than hear one any day.

I'd rather one would walk with me—than merely show the way.

The eye's a better pupil—more willing than the ear,

Fine counsel is confusing, but example's always clear.

And the best of all the people are the ones who live their creed,

For to see the good in action is what everybody needs.

I can soon learn how to do it if you'll let me see it done.

I can watch your hands in action, but your tongue too fast may
	run.

The lectures you deliver may be very wise and true—

But I'd rather get my lesson by observing what you do.

Example is not the main thing in life—it is the only thing. —Albert Schweitzer

☺

For I may misunderstand you, and the high advice you give,

But there's no misunderstanding how you act and how you live.[4]

Our examples should be like a beacon of light, leading our kids down the road of godly living. Jesus tells us, "In the same way, let your light shine before men, that they may see your good deeds and praise your Father in heaven" (Matthew 5:16). As our lights shine for Christ, may our children see our good deeds and praise the Lord—with their words and with their lives.

POWER POINT

Read: 1 Corinthians 4:16–17 and 10:31–11:1. What kind of example did Paul set for those who followed him? Can you confidently proclaim with him, "Follow my example, as I follow the example of Christ"?

Pray: Blessed Lord, you are the perfect example of righteousness. I love you and want to live for you as an example of goodness and godliness in my home. I recognize that I need you. I cannot live an exemplary life on my own. Help me each day, by the power of your Spirit within me, to honor you with my actions and words. Thank you for your help, your loving kindness, and your forgiveness. In Jesus' name I pray. Amen.

Do: Write a one-paragraph description of the example you want to set for your family. You may want to use Galatians 5:22–23 or Colossians 3:12–14 as references. Put this paragraph by your prayer journal and ask God to help you live out this description of a good role model.

Making Marvelous Memories
Creating Lasting Traditions in Your Family

Make a memory with your children,
Spend some time to show you care;
Toys and trinkets can't replace those
Precious moments that you share.
—Elaine Hardt

Before you begin this chapter, I want you to get comfortable. Make yourself a cup of tea. Sink down deep into that chair. Adjust the pillows. Put your feet up.

Now think back to some of your fondest childhood memories. Go ahead, take as much time as you want. Which recollections bring a smile to your face and a warm feeling to your heart? For some women, the best memories are of family vacations and other adventures embarked upon with parents and siblings. For others, the best memories are of holiday celebrations or special birthday parties. Still others would say their most precious memories are of sitting around the dinner table in the evenings, enjoying family meals and interesting conversation.

Special times such as these have woven a tapestry of unforgettable moments into our lives, and we are the richer for it. Now we are the parents, and it is our turn to create memorable moments for *our* kids. What we do with our children over the next few years—the fun that we have and the memories we make—will broaden their horizons, enrich their lives, and prepare them to pass on special traditions to their families for generations to come.

Of course, as we seek to make memories for our children, we mustn't try *too* hard. Sometimes we can become so focused on our efforts to create memories for the future that we fail to enjoy the present! A family tradition can't be forced. In fact, we can ruin a potential family memory by our overzealous efforts to make sure everything is "just right."

Consider one mother—we'll call her Sheila—who came up with what she thought would be a great family tradition. Each spring she ferried her kids to the mall to have their pictures taken on the special Easter train on display in the center court. When the children were toddlers, the "Kodak moment" was great fun for all, and Sheila determined that she would continue the tradition. Her plan was to have a complete collection of framed photos of the kids on the train from ages one to eighteen.

The idea went well while the children were young and easy to manage; but as they grew into preadolescence, they began to balk. What if one of their friends saw them sitting on a kiddie ride? From that point on, a battle erupted each spring when Sheila planned the trip to the mall. Finally she dropped the idea altogether. She realized she was making a memory—but it wasn't the positive one she had anticipated!

Fond memories are born out of pleasant experiences. As we explore ways to build traditions within our families, we must always remember that our goal is to leave wonderful impressions on the minds of our children. If our attempt to create a memory feels forced, it is not likely to have the desired impact.

I'm reminded of a particular woman who was preparing for a dinner party. She was so distracted by the cooking, cleaning, and other preparations that she was unable to give attention to her guests, including the guest of honor. Perhaps you recognize this woman as Martha in the New Testament. She missed the point of having everyone in her home—which was to enjoy the company of good friends. Her sister

Mary, however, seized the moment and enjoyed the relationships. Similarly, we can easily miss the point of creating memorable moments if we are focused on the wrong objective. If we build on our relationships and celebrate the times we have together; wonderful memories will overflow as a result.

In this chapter, I want to share with you some practical ways to celebrate life as it happens. Allow these ideas to spur your own creativity as you think of more ways to develop meaningful family traditions. Happy living!

Unforgettable Birthdays

Once a year each of our children have their special day—their birthday. Birthdays are a time for them to be honored and to feel that they are not only important, they are extraordinary! We can assist our kids in having an unforgettable day by being a little creative. For example:

The Plate of Honor. Buy a bright red plate, or make a special plate with supplies from a craft store. In the middle, write something like "You're Special!" or "It's Your Day!" Then store it away, only bringing it out on a family member's birthday. Serve all of their meals that day on the Plate of Honor. Then put the plate back in the cupboard until the next family birthday.

Favorite Meals. Several days before a birthday, ask the birthday child what he or she would like to have for breakfast, lunch, and dinner. Then go the extra mile to provide those favorite meals on that special day.

Birthday Parties. Creative parties can make wonderful, lifelong memories. You may want to do a party every year or every other year (depending on your sanity level). But planning a party is not as difficult as you might think. Start by coming up with a theme—something that corresponds with your child's interests. You can build a theme around anything your child loves—baseball, fire trucks, teddy bears, you name it! Look in craft stores and party books for ideas for age-appropriate games, crafts, and activities. Allow the birthday child to be a part of the planning process as he or she gets to be a little older. You will find great joy in planning an event together. My kids continue to remember and talk about their favorite parties throughout the years.

Spiritual Birthdays. Just as you celebrate a physical birthday, you can also celebrate a spiritual birthday. The event of spiritual rebirth is described by Jesus in John 3:3–15 as a time when we decide to put our faith in Jesus Christ as God's son and our savior. What a wonderful day to remember and celebrate year after year! Rejoice together as a family as you bring out the Plate of Honor and perhaps present a special, heartfelt gift to the honoree.

Heavenly Holidays

Holidays offer a multitude of opportunities to carry on old traditions and begin new ones. As each holiday approaches, take time to deliberately introduce at least one new tradition. If it is well accepted and everyone has fun, write it down and plan to continue it in the years to come. A "Holiday Traditions Journal" is a splendid way for you to record your ideas and help you remember the best ones from year to year. Later the journal can be copied and passed down from generation to generation. Include in the journal your family's favorite holiday recipes as well as traditions you have carried on from years past.

Here are a few fun suggestions for the holidays, from January through December:

New Year's Day

- Eat black-eyed peas and corn bread as you watch football together. Choose different teams for each of you to cheer on.

Keep tally of the scores, and award a funny prize to the family member who racks up the most points during the day.

- Pray together for the New Year and for each individual in the family.

- Have everyone write goals or resolutions and share them with the rest of the family.

- Make popcorn and watch a movie, or play a board game together.

- Write a "Here's Hoping" list. Ask each family member to contribute one idea of something fun he or she would like to do during the coming year. Try to set some dates for when these ideas could be carried out.

Valentine's Day

- Cut heart shapes from red or pink paper and ask your family members to write kind, appreciative notes to each of the other people in the family. Deliver the notes at the dinner table.

- Read a love story together or retell the story of how you and your husband met. Pull out your wedding album and tell your children about each of the pictures.

- Make heart sandwiches for lunch using heart-shaped cookie cutters to cut out the bread.

- Have the whole family wear red or pink all day.

- Get together with your kids to cook Dad's favorite dessert.

- Think of one way your family could show God's love to others in the community. Make a plan to carry it out together.

St. Patrick's Day

- Give your child a green bracelet or ring to wear each year only on St. Patrick's Day. Keep it in a special green box that you bring out on that morning.

- Serve green food and drinks. A little food coloring can go a long way to make green eggs, green cookies, green biscuits, and much more.

- Read the story about St. Patrick together.

- Eat green lollipops and have a contest to see who has the greenest tongue.

- Hunt for four-leaf clovers. Talk about God's plan for each of your children's lives, and explain why trusting God is different than believing in luck.

Easter

- Read the Easter story in Luke 24 in the Bible. Talk with your children about the hope we have in Jesus.

- Take communion together as a family and explain the symbolism of each element.

- Hard boil and decorate eggs together. Explain that the eggs symbolize new life, and that's what we're celebrating at Easter—our new life in Christ. If you want to go further, you can also note that the egg has three parts, reminding us of the Trinity: the hard outer shell (God, our refuge); the egg white (Jesus, our purifier); and the yolk (the Holy Spirit, our nourishment).

- Make Easter cookies together, then take them to someone you and the kids want to tell about Jesus.

- Attend a sunrise service together at a local church.

- Prepare an Easter egg hunt using plastic eggs that open at the middle. Fill them with coins, candy, or notes that tell some part of the Easter story. Encourage the kids to try to find enough eggs to put together the whole account.

Fourth of July

- Plan a neighborhood parade. Encourage everyone to decorate their bikes, trikes, and strollers and march together through the neighborhood. Use a boom box to provide patriotic music and serve refreshments when the parade is done.

- Invite several families over for hot dogs on the grill and to watch fireworks. Try to include the same families every year.

- Read a short biographical sketch about one of our nation's founding fathers. Read several famous quotes by this person too.

- Fly your flag and make a ceremony of putting it up and taking it down. Have the kids set small flags in the ground to "decorate" your yard.

Thanksgiving

- Allow each child to pick one favorite recipe for the Thanksgiving meal and have him or her assist you in making it. Proudly tell the guests who helped make each dish.

- Decorate the dinner table together with the kids. Use colorful leaves and acorns from your yard to accent the centerpiece on the table.

- Make a "Gratitude" poster or tablecloth. Write the words "I am thankful for…" across the top of a large poster board and ask everyone to add their thoughts. Read them out loud at the end of the Thanksgiving meal. Or purchase a white cotton tablecloth and allow your guests to sign it, adding their thoughts of gratitude and the date. Bring out the tablecloth year after year.

- Read the story of the first Thanksgiving, or read the Thanksgiving Proclamation given by George Washington or Abraham Lincoln.

- Set five kernels of corn at each place setting. Tell the story of how the Pilgrims did the same thing at the first Thanksgiving in remembrance and gratitude for how God brought them through a terrible winter—a season so bad that for a few days they had only a day's ration of five corn kernels to eat.

Christmas

- Have a caroling party with all the kids in the neighborhood.

- Help a family in need by visiting them, giving them gifts, and praying with them.

- Read about the Christmas traditions from the land of your heritage. Choose one you may want to start in your own family.

- Decorate the house and the Christmas tree together. Make sure everyone pitches in! Play your favorite Christmas music and serve hot cocoa.

- Set out a small box and put thin strips of paper beside it. Tell your family members that every time they notice someone in the family doing a kind deed for another person, they are to write it down on a strip of paper and put it in the box. Hopefully, by Christmas day the box will be full. Explain that the box represents Christ's manger, and the kind deeds are the straw laid in preparation for his arrival.

- Set aside one day as a baking day, and have the kids help with the stirring, the mixing, and the licking of spoons. Together, take the cookies, breads, cakes, and pies as gifts to the neighbors.

- Choose one night to drive around and look at the Christmas lights on the houses in your community. Eat Christmas cookies as you go.

- After the Christmas Eve service, invite one family over for tamales and chili.

- Give the kids a new pair of Christmas pajamas on Christmas Eve.

- Give only three gifts to your children, just as Jesus received three gifts.

- Read the Christmas story from Luke 2 and talk about God's gift to the world before you begin to open gifts on Christmas morning.

- Have a green and red breakfast. At our house, we traditionally have green eggs and ham, plus a cherry coffeecake. My family insists on it every year now!

Therefore, brethren, stand fast and hold the traditions which you were taught, whether by word or our epistle. —2 Thessalonians 2:15 NKJV

Two More Significant Days

If your children are school-age, there are two special days which are fun to recognize. They don't fall in the "holiday" category, but they are significant just the same: the beginning of summer vacation and the first day of school. These days loom large to all students, whether they are home-schooled or attend a public or private school. Here are some thoughts on making these days memorable:

Beginning of Summer

- Throw a family party on the first day of summer vacation. Decorate the house with balloons, provide your kids' favorite junk food, and celebrate their achievements from the year.

- Make a summer planning poster. Write across the top "Summer 2001" (or whatever year it is). Then make a list of fun activities you and kids want to do over the next two months. Also include some summer rules, such as how much television time will be allowed, what chores will be required, and how late is too late to sleep in.

- Make a "Boredom Busters" can. Cover a coffee can with construction paper and decorate it with stickers and the words "Boredom Busters." Sit down with the kids and talk about activities they can do when they feel bored. Remind them that "boredom is in the eyes of the beholder" and there is always something to do if they will use their imaginations. Have them each contribute five ideas to the can. If they say they're bored in the weeks that follow, tell them to reach into the can and pull out a "boredom buster."

- Plan several one-day field trips together—to the park, the beach, the zoo, the museum, or other places of interest.

- Provide one interesting workbook for them to do to keep mentally alert. You might want to have an incentive system to motivate them. Or provide an incentive for them to read a good book or two. A new computer program may also be a hit.

- Appeal to their creative bent by providing a new sketch pad, paint set, or musical instrument to take up during the summer.

First Day of School

- Take a picture of the kids at the front door of your home with schoolbooks in hand.

- Make each child's favorite lunch to take to school. Tuck in a special note telling them how proud you are of them.

- Set a scholastic goal for the coming year, such as a certain grade point average or all As and Bs.

- Plan a special snack for after school—or maybe a trip to the ice-cream shop.

- Establish a new work area and study schedule to fit your child's needs. Buy new pens, pencils, and paper for the work area.

- Pray together about the school year. Start a prayer journal or prayer calendar for the year, keeping a record of prayer requests and answers to prayer.

- At dinner, ask each child to tell one thing they like about their new teacher. Encourage them to talk about their day and their friends.

Travel Traditions

Several years ago our family took a short trip to the hill country of Texas. We decided to go exploring down the country roads in our car and came upon a small mountain called Enchanted Rock—a large, granite mount with smooth sides situated in the middle of a state park. Venturing into the park, we noticed that people were climbing up the mountain, so we decided to get out of the car and try the climb too. When we reached the top with only a minimal struggle, we felt victorious. We could see for miles around in every direction, and we were awestruck by the natural beauty of the area.

We got the camera out and took pictures, then decided to descend the rock by a different route. Oops! Trying to find a safe passage down was a bigger challenge than we expected. At times my husband, Curt, had to help the girls and me leap across small crevasses and slide down steep inclines. When we finally managed to make it to the bottom, we rejoiced, knowing that we had succeeded together in a difficult task. We still remember that climb to this day—what a challenge it was and how we helped and encouraged each other along the way. We didn't spend a lot of money to make this memory, nor did we plan for it to happen. But we experienced a special bond, and none of us will ever forget it.

That's what family trips do—they bond family members together and provide opportunities for unforgettable moments. How can you make the most of these traveling adventures? Consider incorporating some of the following traditions into your next travel plan:

Goodie Bag. Put together a small goodie bag for each child with age-appropriate activities, plus snacks and drinks. Books, markers, paper, and small games make good items for the bag. Wait to give the child his or her goodie bag until just before you get on the plane or into the car. My kids look forward to the start of every trip because they love their special bags.

Family Photographer. Designate one family member as the photographer for the trip. Older kids will take great pride in this job. Explain that these will be the photos that will go into the family photo album. When you return, create your photo album quickly so that the task doesn't hang over your head. Get the kids to help. Leave the photo album on the coffee table for several weeks so that everyone can look at it and reflect on the trip.

Travel Video. Designate another family member to create a video record of the trip as you go along. At the end of the vacation, interview each family member on tape and ask them to name their five best memories of the trip. Choose one night to eat popcorn and watch the video.

Mystery Game Bag. Put several small travel games or puzzles in a pillowcase (one for each evening you are on the trip). Before dinner each night, allow one family member to blindly pick one item out of the bag. That game or puzzle can then be played while waiting for your meal at a restaurant or after dinner in the hotel room. Save the games for future trips.

On-the-Way-Home Poem. Coming home from a great getaway can be a downer for everyone. Why not use the travel time to reflect on your journey? Ask each person in the family to list some of their favorite moments. Then, working together, create a family poem about the trip. It can be silly or serious! When you get home, type up the poem and frame it with a photograph from the getaway. Begin a "Wall of Memories" in a hallway in your house.

Passing It On

Passing on traditions from generation to generation is not just great fun; it is important. In the Old Testament, God often instructed his people to pass their traditions from one generation to the next in the form of special feasts. The Passover feast, for example, represents the Israelites' exodus from Egypt, when the angel of death "passed over" those Jewish homes that had the blood of a lamb sprinkled on their doorposts. To this day, Jewish families observe this feast and remember God's faithfulness and redemption. The Passover—and other great feasts and celebrations proscribed in the Bible—not only continue to bring families together in unity and worship, they illustrate spiritual truths and point ultimately to the Messiah.

We, too, are blessed by the traditions and celebrations we pass down through our families. Our children learn to celebrate life and appreciate God's faithfulness through the celebrations and traditions we teach them while they're young. It is not enough to tell them how life should be lived; we must live it abundantly ourselves each day, passing on our ideas, hopes, and dreams. We must teach our kids how to celebrate life through our own example.

This year holds incredible potential for making memories with your family! As a positive mom, start today to celebrate life—and watch with joy as your children celebrate with you.

POWER POINT

Read: Leviticus 23, where God describes the various feasts that the Israelites were to observe. Notice the traditions God set forth for his people and consider the memories he intended to establish.

Pray: Mighty and awesome God, thank you for your loving care over my family. Thank you for your son, Jesus, whom we should celebrate every day. Help me to be faithful to pass on traditions and celebrations that honor you and celebrate life. Help me to build positive memories in the lives of my children—especially ones that help them reflect on your constant love and faithfulness. Help me to live life abundantly in you. In Jesus' name I pray. Amen.

Do: Begin a "Family Traditions Journal" using a blank notebook. Record old and new traditions for each holiday. Add recipes and other ideas you collect over the years. (One day, as a wedding present to your children, make a copy of the book so that they have some family traditions to pass on to their own kids.)

Principle #6

THe Power of

OF

Strong Moral Standards

*The intergenerational poverty that troubles us so much today
is predominantly a poverty of values.*
—Dan Quayle

Whoever would love life
and see good days
must keep his tongue from evil
and his lips from deceitful speech.
He must turn from evil and do good;
he must seek peace and pursue it.
For the eyes of the Lord are on the righteous
and his ears are attentive to their prayer,
but the face of the Lord is against those who do evil.
—1 Peter 3:10–12

Living by the Book
Anchoring Your Children in God's Word

In regard to this Great Book, I have but to say, I believe the Bible is the best gift God has given to man. All the good Savior gave to the world was communicated through this Book. But for this Book we could not know right from wrong. All things most desirable for man's welfare, here and hereafter, are to be found portrayed in it.
—Abraham Lincoln

In October 1998 the Guadalupe River in South Texas swelled far beyond its banks and grew into a massive torrent of rushing water, carrying away every object in its path. Susan Foster, one of the survivors of the flood, describes her experience:

About forty feet of water swept over our entire seven acres like a tidal wave. All that remains looks like a war zone—no windows or doors. Even the cedar logs (one foot in diameter and fourteen feet long) which were buried three feet into the ground with concrete were either snapped off or pulled out. Thankfully the first floor is made of cast-in-place bridge concrete pillars. Otherwise our house would have vanished like so many others.... Washing machines and refrigerators made hasty exits through walls and windows, as did all of the furniture.... I did find one chair about one-half mile down the river, although it was thirty feet up in a tree! One man's engraved bowling ball was found over one hundred miles down stream.[1]

Clearly, the powerful current of a raging river can be overwhelmingly destructive. As we see from Susan's account, only those things that are firmly anchored have a chance of withstanding such forceful turbulence. My heart truly goes out to families in the wake of a flood!

But while a flood like the one Susan described will make headline news for days, another flood that continues to destroy lives every day never seems to make it into the mainstream press. I'm talking about our society's destructive moral current that is flowing rapidly downstream. These raging waters quickly and easily sweep over young and impressionable hearts and minds. Only those children who are properly anchored have a chance of surviving such a strong, dominating current.

From the Internet to Hollywood to magazines at the checkout stands, immoral images and corrupting information swirl around our families. Gone are the days when purity was valued, human life was respected, and God was almost unanimously reverenced. The tide has shifted to a sexually open and perverse society that devalues human life through violence and abortion and makes God and his followers the object of derision. Although years ago the name of God was honored and revered even by unbelievers, now Christians are the subjects of jokes, and God himself is portrayed as a goofy cartoon character on prime time television!

Christian apologist Josh McDowell describes the seriousness of our moral decline this way: "I believe that one of the prime reasons this generation is setting new records for dishonesty, disrespect, sexual promiscuity, violence, suicide and other pathologies is because they have lost their moral underpinnings; their foundational belief in morality and truth has been eroded."[2] How true! The pervasive mind-set today is "Whatever you think is right, is right." No absolutes. Just make your own rules for life. If it feels good, do it. With this kind of philosophy, a young person is little more than a house of cards in the path of the floodwaters; he or she will be carried off easily by the thoughts and ideas of this world—and will likely meet destruction along the way.

As positive moms, we can protect our kids from some influences, but we can't control everything that goes into their minds. We can't insulate them completely from the world's way of thinking. If they are school age, they are away from us a good part of most days. Even if they are home-schooled, they are likely to see or hear things at times that we wish they didn't. But while we might not be able to prevent every worldly thought from getting into their impressionable heads, we can give them a foundation of moral truth on which to stand—a solid rock that will not only keep their heads above the water but will give them the strength and courage to stem the tide.

That foundation is the Word of God. The Bible offers timeless truths for us to pass on to our children. The standards set forth in Scripture are not just a set of rules and regulations, but instructions for a joyful and fulfilling life. If we will faithfully teach the truths of the Bible and assist our kids in living out these precepts, they will have an anchor in the flood and a sure foundation. Jesus used a parable to illustrate this concept in Luke 6:47–49:

> I will show you what he is like who comes to me and hears my words and puts them into practice. He is like a man building a house who dug down deep and laid the foundation on rock. When a flood came, the torrent struck that house but could not shake it, because it was well built. But the one who hears my words and does not put them into practice is like a man who built a house on the ground without a foundation. The moment the torrent struck that house, it collapsed, and its destruction was complete.

Perhaps you are familiar with the children's song using this parable. If you could hear the sound of my voice, I'd sing it to you: "The foolish man built his house on the sand. When the rains came down and the floods came up, the house on the sand went *SMASH!*" Point well taken! How are we building the houses of our lives? Are we laying a sure foundation by hearing and doing God's Word? What about the foundation we're laying for our kids? Are we raising them on the solid rock of the Scriptures so they are anchored to withstand the current trends of a rapidly declining morality?

Taming the Barbarian

Dr. Albert Siegel said in the *Stanford Observer,* "When it comes to rearing children, every society is only twenty years away from barbarism. Twenty years is all we have to accomplish the task of civilizing the infants who are born into our midst each year. These savages know nothing of our language, our culture, our religion, our values, our customs of interpersonal relations…. The barbarian must be tamed if civilization is to survive."[3] Now, we may not consider our children barbarians or savages (well, there are times!), but we can't argue that they need direction, training, and discipline. As positive moms, we must take the initiative to teach God's principles to our kids. Civilization may very well be at stake!

How do we effectively teach God's Word? In chapter 15 we discussed the importance of setting a good example with our actions and words. Setting an example of devotion to Scripture is part of that responsibility. Our young observers need to see us pouring over God's Word, enjoying its blessings and applying its truths in our lives. Remember, kids are copycats! But modeling a love for the Bible is not enough. We must also have a deliberate plan of instruction. We must set aside a time and a place to teach our children about the Bible. Taking them to church is helpful, but we should not depend on one hour a week in Sunday school for their entire biblical upbringing.

Parents, after all, have the main responsibility to pass on God's foundational truths to their kids. God tells his people in Deuteronomy 6:6–8, "These commandments that I give you today are to be upon our hearts. Impress them on your children. Talk about them when you sit at home and when you walk along the road, when you lie down and when you get up. Tie them as symbols on your hands and bind them on your foreheads. Write them on the doorframes of your houses and on your gates."

The point is we should always be looking for opportunities to teach our kids the Word of God! We can talk about the Bible:

- Around the breakfast table

- In the car, on the way to school or activities

- In the car, on the way home from school or activities

- During dinner

- Over dessert

- At bedtime

Anytime is a good time to teach the principles of God's Word. Decide what is best for your family, then do it!

How do you start? Perhaps your family would enjoy reading together some of the Psalms or Proverbs, or perhaps one of the Gospels. You might want to purchase one of the many excellent, age-appropriate devotional books available at Christian bookstores. Whatever you choose, begin the habit of reading and enjoying God's Word together as soon as possible, preferably while your kids are young. Set the example early.

As your children grow and mature (say, by about the age of eight or ten), encourage them to begin developing their own personal devotional time. Invest in a youth Bible or other easy-to-read translation. Give them a blank journal, a special highlighter pen, and an age-appropriate devotional plan. Help them to establish a time each day when they can read the Bible and pray. Ask them about some of the truths they are learning; use open-ended questions such as "Can anyone share a miracle they read about this week in God's Word?"

In our home, the dinner hour has become an important time to talk about current events, social issues, and biblical truths. Now and then I like to bring out an interesting devotional book—like *Sticky Situations* by Betsy Schmitt (Tyndale House) or *Courageous Christians* by Joyce Vollmer Brown (Moody)—to help get the family talking. My personal favorite (because I wrote it!) is *Table Talk* (Broadman & Holman Publishers), which includes discussion questions for young and old alike along with correlating Bible verses. Another good discussion starter I found recently is *God—Seen through the Eyes of the Greatest Minds* (Howard Publishing). This book provides interesting quotes about God from renowned scientists, philosophers, artists, musicians, and writers throughout history.

Another good idea is to memorize scripture verses together as a family. Write the memory verse on a poster, chalkboard, or white board for all family members to see. Set a time limit for memorizing the verse and offer a reward for everyone who achieves the goal. Write notes to your kids, encouraging them with Bible verses to help them see how God's Word can be applied day to day. You will find that as your family works together to memorize Scripture and apply it to daily life, your kids' interest in the great Instruction Book for Life will deepen and grow.

A Great American Example

George Washington stands out in history as one of America's greatest heroes. His integrity and leadership led this nation through its challenging formative years. Certainly God's hand was upon our nation's first president, but George Washington also credits another important

How can a young man keep his way pure? By living according to your word. I seek you with all my heart; do not let me stray from your commands. —Psalm 119:9–10

person in his life for his success. Consider what he had to say about his mother: "My mother was the most beautiful woman I ever saw. All that I am I owe to my mother. I attribute all my success in life to the moral, intellectual, and physical education I received from her."[4] What made Mary Ball Washington so influential in the life of her son?

Widowed when George was only eleven years old, Mary was a devoted Christian who earnestly desired to glorify God in the way she raised her children. One historian writes, "In addition to instruction in the Bible and Prayer Book, which were her daily companions, it was Mrs. Washington's custom to read some helpful books to her children at home, and in this way they received much valuable instruction."[5]

One of the books she read to her children was *Contemplations, Moral and Divine* by Sir Matthew Hale, which contained devotional writings that taught biblical principles and gave advice on living a moral and godly life. It is no wonder that as we read George's own writings, we see a man of sincere faith and humble, godly leadership. In his personal prayer book, consisting of twenty-four handwritten prayers, we catch a glimpse of this mighty man's genuine heart:

MONDAY MORNING... O eternal and everlasting God, I presume to present myself this morning before Thy Divine Majesty, beseeching Thee to accept of my humble and hearty thanks.... Direct my thoughts, words and work, wash away my sins in the immaculate Blood of the Lamb, and purge my heart by Thy Holy Spirit.... Daily frame me more and more into the likeness of Thy Son, Jesus Christ, that living in Thy fear, and dying in Thy favor, I may in Thy appointed time attain the resurrection of the just unto eternal life. Bless my family, friends and kindred, and unite us all in praising and glorifying Thee in all our works.[6]

Are you as inspired as I am by Mary Ball Washington's example of faithful, fervent, and diligent teaching of God's Word? I know that as I read her son's prayer, I am motivated to elevate the teaching of the Scriptures to my children to the top priority it deserves.

Passing the Baton

In my first few years as a teacher, I served as the assistant track coach. One of my favorite events at the track meets was the 4 x 100-meter relay. This race is quick and competitive, but running is only a part. Victory rides on the proper handoff of the baton from one runner to the next. If the handoff is not right, the baton is dropped, and the race is lost! In nearly every meet I attended, I saw at least one team drop the baton and fall behind the rest of the pack. I made sure our runners practiced the handoff over and over again so they wouldn't make a mistake when it really counted.

As positive moms, we have a baton to hand off to the next generation in the form of strong moral standards. It is our job to practice the handoff over and over again so that when it really counts, the transition is seamless, and victory is achieved in our children's lives.

I believe four elements are crucial in the makeup of that moral baton. The first is found in Matthew 22:37–40: "Love the Lord your God with all your heart and with all your soul and with all your mind. This is the first and greatest commandment. And the second is like it; Love your neighbor as yourself. All the Law and the Prophets hang on these two commandments." Memorize these verses with your children, then show them how to live them out each day.

Second, teach your kids the Ten Commandments. While these represented God's moral standards for the Israelites in the Old Testament, they are still important precepts for godly living today. You will find them in Exodus 20.

From there, move on to other passages in Scripture that teach how to relate to the world and the people around us—for example, Romans 12, Colossians 3, and Matthew 5, 6, and 7 (known as the Sermon on the Mount). Of course, God's character and principles for living are revealed throughout the Scriptures, so don't limit yourself to these passages.

Finally, teach your children courage by studying the lives of biblical heroes. Courage is a key character trait our kids will definitely need to live godly, moral lives in an immoral world. Courage to stand alone. Courage to stand up for what is right. Courage to do what is right when everyone else is doing wrong.

When my husband was in college (a Christian university, in fact), his biology professor opened the first class with the question, "Is there anyone here who does not believe in evolution?" Curt was the only student who stood up and said, "I believe in the creation/intelligent design plan presented in the Book of Genesis." Perhaps other students in that classroom agreed with Curt, but none had the courage to stand up and be counted.

In today's schools, it can be even harder for Christian students to stand up for what they believe. Fortunately the Bible is full of stories of courageous men and women who faced difficult odds but relied on God's strength to see them through—people like Deborah, Moses, Joshua, Esther, David, Daniel, Peter, and Paul. Help your kids to learn and be inspired by their examples. Memorize Joshua 1:9 with them: "Have I not commanded you? Be strong and courageous. Do not be terrified; do not be discouraged, for the LORD your God will be with you wherever you go."

I am so thankful for God's Word, aren't you? The Bible is a strong and steady anchor for life—the only sure foundation in a world that's teetering on shifting sand. We need that foundation. Our children need that foundation. The world, whether it knows it or not, needs us to have that foundation! Today let's commit to faithfully pass the baton of the knowledge of God and his Word to the next generation. As we do, we'll show the world the power of a positive mom.

POWER POINT

Read: Psalm 119. Notice David's love and devotion to God's Word. Memorize a verse from this psalm that is particularly meaningful to you.

Pray: Mighty and majestic God of the universe, I praise your name. You are powerful, faithful, and just! Help me to honor you with my life and in my home. Help me to be faithful to teach my children the principles of righteous living that you have given in your Word. Show me how to teach effectively. Help me to reach the next generation for you and glorify you through everything I do as a mother. In Jesus' name, amen.

Do: Visit a Christian bookstore and purchase a children's devotional that fits the needs of your family. Then prayerfully plan a time each day when you will teach your children truths from God's Word. Be consistent, but don't get frustrated if you miss a time now and then. Keep everything age-appropriate, upbeat, and relatively brief so that your kids will look forward to your teaching times together and grow to love and understand God's Word.

Legacies in Literature
Teaching Character through History and the Classics

With the loss of tradition we have lost the thread which safely guided us through the vast realms of the past, but this thread was also the chain fettering each successive generation to a predetermined aspect of the past. It could be that only now will the past open up to us with unexpected freshness and tell us things that no one as yet had ears to hear.
—Hannah Arendt

Recently I purchased a book entitled *How to Think like Leonardo da Vinci* by Michael J. Gelb. I have always been fascinated by da Vinci and jumped at the chance to explore this legendary man's thought processes. I'm thankful for people like him who provide wonderful examples of courage and creativity to us all.

We need not look far to find heroes in history and in literature who teach us about life through their mistakes as well as their achievements. As positive moms, we can reach back in time and grab these stories, fables, tales, and biographies to share with our children, teaching them important lessons for their lives and their futures. As we help them develop a love for history and literature, we open up to them new worlds of opportunity to learn and grow and be enriched. They gain so much—and we do too—when we open this door of wisdom into the hearts and minds of those who went before us.

With good books as their guide, our children can explore exotic islands, parched deserts, busy subways, dark jungles, and raging rapids. They can learn how to live lives of spiritual passion and courage from the examples they see in books of brave men, resourceful women, daring adventurers, enthusiastic children, and compassionate friends. They can even learn how *not* to live from the bad examples they see of cruel teachers, unwise leaders, lazy workers, and disobedient kids.

Good resources are plentiful—you just need to know where to find them. So how and where do we start? What books are best for kids of different ages? How do we motivate our kids to read?

I'm reminded of the young mother who once asked a minister, "At what age should I begin the education of my child?"

"Madam," came the reply, "from the very first smile that gleans over an infant's cheeks, your opportunity begins."[1]

We can begin to read to our children from the moment they are born; in fact, some experts say we should begin reading to them *before* they are born since they can hear their mother's voice in the womb! Although they may not understand what the words mean, by beginning the practice of lovingly reading to our children even in infancy, we establish a routine and an interest in their impressionable minds. Soon they will recognize the rhythm and flow of poetry and nursery rhymes. They will want stories repeated over and over as they enjoy the warm embrace of our voices and the familiarity of the tales. Then, in their preschool years, we can begin to focus on establishing a pattern of reading and listening, helping our children learn to love and be attentive to stories and poems.

Gleaning from the Greats

Familiarity with classics in literature allows our children to expand their understanding of everyday communication. When young people hear the term "cry wolf," they will understand the meaning only if they've read or heard of the classic Aesop's fable. Only after reading or listening to the story of King Midas will they understand that the

"Midas touch" describes someone who has the ability to turn everything he or she touches into gold or success.

More importantly, with a knowledge and understanding of literature comes the opportunity for our kids to learn lessons from the characters in the stories. For example, the story of "The Ugly Duckling" presents a wonderful lesson about accepting people for who they are and not rejecting them on the basis of their appearance. Charles Dickens's *A Christmas Carol* shows the power of repentance and the importance of caring for others. The tales of King Arthur and the knights of the Round Table teach bravery, courage, chivalry, and devotion to God. *The Swiss Family Robinson* by Yohann Rudolf Wyss demonstrates the strength of a family working together to overcome difficult odds.

William J. Bennett, in his book *The Educated Child*, puts it this way: "Never underestimate the power of literature to teach good character. Stories and poems can help children see what virtues and vices look like. They offer heroes to emulate. Their moral lessons lodge in the heart and stay there."[2] The books we read to our kids can act as a confirmation of the values we are teaching them from God's Word.

To get the most from a good book, however, we need to do more than just read. It is important to sum up the reading time with questions such as "Was Peter obedient to his parents? What were the consequences of his disobedience? Why do you think he acted the way he did?" By drawing a conclusion to what was just read, we help our kids learn to think with discernment and clarity. With younger children, we can finish up by summarizing the main point of the story for them; with older children, we can ask them to give a summary in their own words.

Linda Karges-Bone, assistant professor of education at Charleston Southern University, says that parents can begin to introduce stories rich in value and content when their kids are about seven years old. She

My son, preserve sound judgment and discernment; do not let them out of your sight; they will be life for you, an ornament to grace your neck. —Proverbs 3:21–22

encourages parents to ask themselves the following ten questions when evaluating the worth of a book for their children (my paraphrase):

1. Has the author's work stood the test of time?

2. Did a reputable company publish the book?

3. Does the description on the book cover indicate a story with a purpose or message?

4. Do words such as "wholesome, values, or thought-provoking" appear on the book jacket or author notes?

5. Has the book won an award, such as the Caldecott Medal or Newberry Award?

6. What does the cover art portray?

7. Is the book written at or just above your child's reading age? It is good to challenge your kids without selecting something that will become drudgery for them.

8. Is the story's theme appropriate for your child? Sensitive topics such as the Holocaust have value but may be difficult for a young child to handle.

9. Do the characters have Christian mind-sets? Many suitable stories show characters behaving in "good ways" without a clear connection to God. Balance these stories with Christian literature, and take the time to discuss each story.

10. Did you preview the book? The extra time is worth the effort.[3]

Here's a list of some of the time-honored favorites to read to your kids or allow them to read when they are ready:

For Preschool and Primary Grades

Aesop for Children, Aesop

Book of Nursery and Mother Goose Rhymes, Marguerite de Angeli

Hans Christian Anderson's Fairy Tales, Hans Christian Anderson

Madeline and other books in the Madeline series, Ludwig Bemelmans

Mike Mulligan and His Steam Shovel and *The Little House,* Virginia Burton

The Courage of Sarah Noble, Alice Dalgleish

John Henry: An American Legend and *The Snowy Day,* Ezra Jack Keats

Pecos Bill, Steven Kellog

Just So Stories, Rudyard Kipling

Frog and Toad Together, Arnold Lobel

Mrs. Piggle-Wiggle, Betty MacDonald

Make Way for Ducklings and *Blueberries for Sal,* Robert McCloskey

Amelia Bedelia, Peggy Parish

Cinderella, Charles Perrault

The Tale of Peter Rabbit, Beatrix Potter

Curious George and other books in the Curious George series, H. A. Rey

A Child's Garden of Verses, Robert Louis Stevenson

The Trumpet of the Swan, E. B. White

The Velveteen Rabbit, Margery Williams

For Intermediate Grades

Little Women, Louisa May Alcott

Sounder, William H. Armstrong

Mr. Popper's Penguins, Richard Atwater

Peter Pan, J. M. Barrie

The Secret Garden, Frances Hodgson Burnett

Johnny Tremain, Esther Forbes

Selections from Poor Richard's Almanack, Benjamin Franklin

The Wind in the Willows, Kenneth Grahame

The Jungle Book and *Captains Courageous*, Rudyard Kipling

The Chronicles of Narnia series, C. S. Lewis

Tales from Shakespeare, Charles and Mary Lamb

A Wrinkle in Time, Madeleine L'Engle

Sarah, Plain and Tall, Patricia Maclachlan

The Borrowers, Mary Norton

Black Beauty, Anna Sewell

Call It Courage, Armstrong Sperry

Heidi, Johanna Spyri

Treasure Island, Robert Louis Stevenson

Charlotte's Web and *Stuart Little*, E. B. White

Little House on the Prairie, Laura Ingalls Wilder

Swiss Family Robinson, Johann Rudolf Wyss

For Older Readers (Age 12 to Young Adult)

Anna Karenina, Leo Tolstoy

Anne Frank: The Diary of a Young Girl, Anne Frank

David Copperfield and *Oliver Twist*, Charles Dickens

Gulliver's Travels, Jonathan Swift

The Illiad and *The Odyssey*, Homer

Jane Eyre, Charlotte Brontë

Kidnapped, Robert Louis Stevenson

The Lord of the Rings trilogy, J. R. R. Tolkien

The Merry Adventures of Robin Hood, Howard Pyle (editor)

Moby Dick, Herman Melville

The Old Man and the Sea, Ernest Hemingway

The Prince and the Pauper, Mark Twain

The Red Badge of Courage, Stephen Crane

Robinson Crusoe, Daniel Defoe

The Scarlet Letter, Nathaniel Hawthorne

The Story of King Arthur and His Knights, Howard Pyle (editor)

20,000 Leagues under the Sea, Jules Verne

The Yearling, Marjorie Kinnan Rawlings

History's Heroes

Like literature, history is a great teacher. "For in history you have a record of the infinite variety of human experience plainly set out for all to see," wrote the Roman historian Livy, "and in that record you can find for yourself and your country both examples and warnings: fine things to take as models, base things, rotten through and through, to avoid."[4] History is rich with pictures of humanity at its best and its worst, and our children grow from the lessons of both. They recognize villains who illustrate bad character as well as heroes who accomplish noble feats. Most importantly, they find that certain truths stand throughout all generations and cultures. They see for themselves that the presence of faith and godly standards help preserve nations and people.

Unfortunately, most modern textbooks downplay or ignore many historical truths that are rooted in biblical faith, replacing them with a revised, "politically correct" record that is both inaccurate and unfriendly to God. As a result, we often must go back to older writings in order to glean from the great lessons history has to offer us. Personally, I enjoy searching for old printed treasures in antique shops. While my husband looks for deals on furniture, I look at the old books! I have found many dated and out-of-print gems that offer delightful and dramatic retellings of history—books such as *When They Were Children: Stories about the Childhood of Great Men and Women* by Amy Steedman, which includes wonderful lessons on faith, courage, perseverance, and character building that we can share with our kids.

Even old textbooks and school readers give us a peek at a history too easily forgotten. As I began to read *McGuffey's Fifth Reader* (the 1879 edition) to my family, I stopped and wept over the beautiful devotion to God expressed in its pages. Our children need to know that our early American forefathers grew up and developed character based on the teaching of God's Word in their classrooms.

Barnes's Elementary History of the United States was a reader used in American schools about a century ago. In the following excerpt about Abraham Lincoln, we are not only reminded of Lincoln's insatiable love for reading, but we see that he aspired to greatness after reading about a hero from history:

> One book that made a great impression on Abe was *Weems's Life of Washington*. He read the story many times. He carried it with him to the field and read it in the intervals of work. Washington was his ideal hero, the one great man whom he admired above all others. Why could not he model his own life after that of the Father of his Country? Why could not he also be a doer of noble deeds and a benefactor of mankind? He might never be President, but he could make himself worthy of that great honor.[5]

Think about it. Abraham Lincoln's reading of history spurred him on to want to be like George Washington! If reading about one of history's heroes could so inspire a young man who lived a simple life in a log cabin, what could it do for our children?

One of my favorite books is *The Light and the Glory* by Peter Marshall and David Manuel. It tells the wonderful, true story of America's godly heritage. I encourage you to read it to your kids, or purchase the children's version so they can read for themselves about the patriotism and faith of our Founding Fathers. *The Book of Virtues* compiled by William J. Bennett is another wonderful resource of literature and history for your entire family to enjoy.

The writings by Washington, Lincoln, and Ben Franklin are interesting family reading, as are good biographies. Again, I prefer to find old biographies from used or antique bookshops because I know they have not been touched by revisionist history.

Providing the Motivation

One lesson we learn from history and experience is that men and women work best when they are properly motivated. When it comes to kids and reading, we would do well to apply this truth in our homes. How can we motivate our children to read some of the marvelous books we bring to them? Try some of the following ideas or mix and match the requirements with different rewards:

- If they read for a certain number of hours during the week, take them out for their favorite meal at a local restaurant or offer some other special activity. Keep a tally of their hours on a chart or chalkboard.

- If they read a certain number of books or pages over a set period of time, provide a monetary reward.

- Allow them to earn television or video game minutes by writing a brief summary about the book they've read.

- For younger kids, adjust the requirement to *listening* to a certain number of books in order to earn their reward—perhaps a trip to their favorite store, reaching into grab bag of goodies, or having a friend over.

Use a chart that you post in the pantry or closet to tally your children's accomplishments. I've found that for school-age kids, this motivation system works best in the summertime, since they are sometimes too busy with their homework during the school year to do extra reading. Still, you can use the time you spend in the car going to and from activities to listen to great literary classics read aloud on tape.

Your efforts, I promise, will be well worth it! In the April 1999 Focus on the Family newsletter, Dr. James Dobson noted six key principles that God has provided as a value system for mankind. They are:

1. Devotion to God

2. Love for others

3. Respect for authority

4. Obedience to divine commandments

5. Self-discipline and self-control

6. Humbleness of spirit

As positive moms, we need to teach our children God's value system using all the resources available to us. The first and foremost resource, of course, is the Bible. But in addition to God's Word, we can supplement our children's education and help them work godly principles into their lives by reading great literature and learning from history. Don't hesitate to start reading to and with your kids. A world of adventure, excitement, and inspiration awaits!

POWER POINT

Read: Proverbs 4. Notice the value Solomon places on listening to instruction and holding on to wisdom. Stories from history and literature bring us wisdom from generations past. Underline all the verses that refer to listening and learning.

Pray: Holy and wonderful Lord, all wisdom and understanding come from you. You are the Creator of all men and women throughout history. Thank you for the opportunity to walk forward into the future having learned from the experiences of others before me. Thank you for the wonderful literature you have provided through the pens of men and women you've inspired. Help me to pass on great truths—your truths—to my children. Help me to raise heroes in the faith within my own family, and thank you for lovingly guiding me in the process. In Jesus' name, amen.

☺ **Do:**   Locate some of the books mentioned in this chapter and begin reading them with your children. Talk about the lessons learned from the stories.

Visit an antique shop and search for old books which tell the stories of great men and women of faith. A book resale shop can also provide a multitude of treasures for your family.

Principle #7

THe Pwer
OF
Love and
Forgiveness

Love is an act of endless forgiveness,
a tender look which becomes a habit.
—Peter Ustinov

*A mother's love is like a circle; it has no beginning and no ending.
It keeps going around and around, always expanding,
touching everyone who comes in contact with it.*
—Art Urban

*Bear with each other and forgive whatever grievances you may have
against one another. Forgive as the Lord forgave you. And over all these
virtues put on love, which binds them all together in perfect unity.*
—Colossians 3:13–14

19

A House of Compassion
How to Sincerely Express Love

Where does love begin? It begins at home. Let us learn to love in our family. In our own family we may have very poor people, and we do not notice them. We have no time to smile, no time to talk to each other. Let us bring that love, that tenderness into our own home and you will see the difference.
—Mother Teresa

At first glance you might think you don't need to read this chapter. Loving your family comes easily to you. It's natural. You're a mother, and love is what mothers do, right?

We are all very familiar with that warm sense of motherly love anchored deep in our hearts for each of our children. But how does that love show itself in our homes? Is it evident in how we treat and speak to our loved ones? It is one thing to proclaim our love for our families and feel it inside; it is another thing to live it out in our daily lives. There are times when we know deep inside that we love our children; but when we are tired and we have just weathered another sibling battle and cleaned up yet another cup of spilled milk, our words and actions may not show it.

I remember a Christmas many years ago when I hired a baby-sitter to play with the kids (then ages three-and-a-half and two) while I went upstairs to a spare bedroom to wrap Christmas presents. It took hours to get all of the packages wrapped just the way I wanted them. When I paid the baby-sitter, I figured it was money well spent.

Several days later, I found myself cooking in the kitchen while the girls played happily upstairs. Suddenly I realized I had heard neither an argument nor a cry for more than forty-five minutes. I hurried up the stairs and noticed small giggles coming from the spare room. You guessed it—my sweet dumplings had gleefully torn the paper off of every present I had so painstakingly wrapped! I must admit my response at that moment was less than loving. In a split second my holiday cheerfulness turned into a winter storm. I wouldn't have wanted anyone to gauge my motherly love based on my words and actions at that moment!

For some mothers, "action" is not the problem. We go through all the motions of what we think is expected of us, day in and day out. But if we're honest with ourselves, we'll admit that we're operating out of duty or guilt or peer pressure or something else. And if our actions are not motivated and accompanied by love, we are spinning our wheels.

Love and action go hand in hand. First Corinthians 13 is considered the "Love Chapter" of the Bible, and in verses 1–3, Paul emphasized the importance of love being evident in our actions:

> If I speak in the tongues of men and of angels, but have not love, I am only a resounding gong or a clanging cymbal. If I have the gift of prophecy and can fathom all mysteries and all knowledge, and if I have a faith that can move mountains, but have not love, I am nothing. If I give all I possess to the poor and surrender my body to the flames, but have not love, I gain nothing.

Romans 12:9 says it another way: "Love must be sincere." What does sincere love look like in word and in deed? In 1 Corinthians 13, Paul provides a description. Read verses 4–7 and see if your love passes the sincerity test. Every time you see the word *love* or *it,* insert your first name:

Love is patient, love is kind. It does not envy, it does not boast, it is not proud. It is not rude, it is not self-seeking, it is not easily angered, it keeps no record of wrongs. Love does not delight in evil but rejoices with the truth. It always protects, always trusts, always hopes, always perseveres.

Now are you convinced that this chapter is worth reading? We all could use a little help, hope, and encouragement in pursuing sincere love for our families. Consider the following personalized version of 1 Corinthians 13:1–7:

1 Corinthians 13 (A Mother's Version)

If I correct your manners at the dinner table, but do not have love, I am only a clanging dinner bell. If I take you for your annual doctor's visit and to story time at the library, and if I stop off at the mall to buy you new shoes, but I have not love, I am nothing. If I give you clean laundry every day and keep the house perfectly straight, but have not love, I gain nothing.

Love kisses the boo-boo before scolding about running in the house. Love encourages creativity instead of worrying about the possible mess. Love carefully disciplines and always forgives. Love doesn't sweat the small stuff. Love smiles and hugs. Love takes the time to look you in the eyes and listen to your side of the story.

Sometimes a mother's love is proclaimed to be unconditional and all-encompassing, closer to God's love for his children than any other love on earth. But love is difficult, even for mothers. A mother's love is much more than that warm feeling that welled up inside of us when we held our babies for the first time. It requires selflessness, patience, and self-control—and a day-in, day-out commitment to demonstrating the sincerity of our love through our actions. No doubt we could all use a few pointers!

What Love Is Not

Before we go any further in our discussion of how to truly love our families, let's establish three things that love is *not:*

1. Love is not letting our kids get away with anything they want to do. As we will learn in the next chapter, if we love our children, we will discipline them. Saying yes to everything a child wants to do is sometimes the easiest course, but it does not show love. On the contrary, we show our kids true love when we set limits and give them boundaries. It takes selfless discipline and strong love to say no when we know what is best for our kids.

2. Love is not giving our children everything they want. In our affluent, fast-paced society, many busy moms feel guilty for not spending enough time with their kids, so they buy them things to make up for their lack of commitment. Other mothers shower their kids with gifts whenever they fly off the handle or lose their tempers, as if presents were apologies. Some divorced moms buy gifts in exchange for being named the "favorite parent." But love does not equal material gifts!

3. Love is also not being a doormat for our children. Some mothers seem to believe that if they truly love, they will allow their kids to take advantage of their selfless actions. No, allowing young people to abuse our selflessness is not a healthy love! There are important boundaries to draw if we want to serve our families with sincere love and also help our children to grow into balanced, self-sufficient adults.

Kerri was a single mom who felt guilty about her divorce and about not spending as much time as she used to with her son, Joey. So when she was home she did everything for Joey, thinking this was a way to show him love. If he was watching TV and said he wanted some ice cream, Kerri would get it. If he didn't like the way his shirt was ironed, she would iron it again. If he wasn't happy with his Christmas gifts, she would take them back and get him exactly what he wanted. Kerri thought that she was loving her son, but instead she was creating a self-centered monster who knew just how to take advantage of his mother!

The Power to Love

Unfortunately, you and I are not capable of producing sincere love in our own strength. We can't demonstrate 1 Corinthians 13 by trying to stir up happy thoughts or warm, fuzzy feelings. We need help. And fortunately, that help is ready and waiting. The Bible says:

> Dear friends, let us love one another, for love comes from God. Everyone who loves has been born of God and knows God. Whoever does not love does not know God, because God is love. This is how God showed his love among us: He sent his one and only Son into the world that we might live through him. This is love: not that we loved God, but that he loved us and sent his Son as an atoning sacrifice for our sins. Dear friends, since God so loved us, we also ought to love one another. No one has ever seen God; but if we love one another, God lives in us and his love is made complete in us. (1 John 4:7–12)

This Scripture passage explains why it is so important for us, as positive moms, to demonstrate sincere love and compassion toward our families: *because this is how they begin to get a glimpse of God's love for them.* No one has seen God. But if we love one another, then the people around us—our families most of all—see a portion of what God's love is like.

These verses also explain how we find the power to love. Sincere love doesn't come from inside us. The Bible tells us that love comes from God, because God is love. The source of love, the essence of love, is not that we loved God, but that he first loved us and sent his son, Jesus, to purchase our salvation through his death on the cross. Now that's love in action! Jesus himself said, "Greater love has no one than this, that he lay down his life for his friends" (John 15:13). God showed us—and continues to show us—the true nature of sincere love.

This is the type of love we are to have for our children. It's a sacrificial love, a love that looks past mistakes and sin and loves even when love isn't deserved. As positive moms, we need to ask God to help us on a daily basis to love our families as he loves—with sincerity, compassion, and mercy. The greatest gift we can give our kids is sincere love that reflects the Father's love for his own children.

Forgive Because You Are Forgiven

Forgiveness is one of the major characteristics of God's love that's absolutely crucial in our homes. Forgiveness does not mean overlooking wrongs that are done, but rather not holding a wrong continually over a family member's head. Remember the story of my kids unwrapping all of the Christmas presents? Can you imagine what that Christmas would have been like in our household if I had continued to grumble and complain and remind the girls of their huge error?

We all know the sense of relief we feel when we are forgiven. Not long ago I was driving to a speaking engagement in Dallas. I was running a bit late (as usual) and not watching my speedometer. Sure enough, just as I was about to pull into the parking lot of the church where I was to speak, I looked in my rearview mirror and saw a policeman on a motorcycle waving at me. I was quite sure he was not just saying hello! I pulled over and rolled down my window.

"Officer, I am so sorry," I said. "I was not paying attention to how fast I was going. I am on my way to speak at that church over there, and I'm running late." Then I added, "By the way, how fast was I going?"

The policeman smiled and assured me that I was going well over the posted speed limit. Then he asked to see my driver's license and proof of insurance (expired of course, since I always forget to put the updated card in the car). He looked up at me and then at the church.

"Okay, go on," he said. "But don't do it again."

A surge of relief ran through my veins. "Thank you, officer," I exclaimed as he walked back to his police car. "I will certainly try!"

That policeman forgave me, even though I didn't deserve it. He offered me mercy when what I deserved was a ticket. We all need mercy, don't we? We all mess up, we disobey, and we live for ourselves. I'm so thankful our heavenly Father forgives us and shows us mercy when we least deserve it!

Forgiveness is a big part of true, sincere love. Psalm 103:8–14 is a beautiful account of God's love, mercy, and forgiveness toward his people:

> The LORD is compassionate and gracious, slow to anger, abounding in love. He will not always accuse, nor will he harbor his anger forever; he does not treat us as our sins deserve or repay us according to our iniquities. For as high as the heavens are above the earth, so great is his love for those who fear him; as far as the east is from the west, so far has he removed our transgressions from us. As a father has compassion on his children, so the LORD has compassion on those who fear him; for he knows how we are formed, he remembers that we are dust.

There are times when our children need mercy, and there are times when our children need punishment. As wise, loving mothers, we must exercise discernment in every situation. If our children deliberately disobey, they must be disciplined in order to learn to be obedient. But if our kids make foolish errors, what they may need is a healthy dose of forgiveness— as I received from the police officer. Let's say my daughter forgets to take

Dear children, let us not love with words or tongue but with actions and in truth. —1 John 3:18

☺

out the garbage because she has been up most of the night studying for a history final. She doesn't deserve mercy, but she needs it! If you and I will be generous with forgiveness toward our children, we will be presenting them with the godly compassion expressed in Psalm 103.

If our children's actions do require punishment, however, we must still follow up that punishment with forgiveness. We can't hold grudges against our kids. Why? Because God forgives us of all of our sins, and we ought to forgive others also. This principle is stated and restated in Scripture numerous times (for example, in Ephesians 4:32 and Colossians 3:13).

Our forgiveness needs to be tempered with loving wisdom, however. Even as we forgive our children, we may need to use caution, withhold a privilege, or follow through with appropriate consequences so that they learn from the experience. Take, for example, a young teenage boy who spends the night at a certain friend's house and is caught sneaking out at night. After punishment and forgiveness, his parents would be wise to employ a healthy caution before allowing him to spend the night at that friend's house again.

Reflecting the Love of God

I love to look at a full moon on a clear night, don't you? Many weary travelers have found their way home by the light of the moon; many lost wanderers have found their path illuminated by its glow. But while a full moon gives off great light, it does not produce the light itself. No, the moon's humble, dusty surface simply reflects the light of the sun. The sun's light is so powerful that even its reflection offers light to all who simply look up!

A mother's love is like the moonlight. The love that pours from her is actually a reflection of the incredible love of our heavenly Father. Do you relish and enjoy his love? Spend some time each day reading his love letter to you—the Bible. As you ponder God's incredible, everlasting love for you, you will begin to shine with his love in your home.

God is love; you and I are simply humble reflectors of love's ultimate source. And just as the moon acts as an instrument of the powerful light of the sun, so we are instruments of God's love to our families. What a privilege! May our loved ones see the continual glow of the Father through us each day!

POWER POINT

Read: Romans 5:1–11. Reflect on the awesome love of God that is poured into our hearts. Memorize Romans 5:8 as a constant reminder of God's demonstration of love to us.

Pray: Great and Holy God, God of love and mercy, I praise you for being the ultimate source of love. Thank you for loving me first and sending your son to purchase my salvation. You show me what sincere love is! Help me to reflect that love in my home, and help my children to learn about your love as they see it reflected in my life. I love you! In Jesus' name I pray. Amen.

Do: Spend some quiet time alone reflecting on God's abundant love for you. Play soft praise music in the background as you read scriptures that remind you of God's love. (You can start with the passages used in this chapter.) Write down a prayer of thanks for his love, mercy, and compassion toward you.

20

Affirmative Training
Disciplining Your Children with Love

*My son, do not despise the LORD's discipline and do not resent
his rebuke, because the LORD disciplines those he loves, as
a father the son he delights in.*
—Proverbs 3:11–12

My first year as a teacher was an education—for me as much
as for my students. I was a seventh-grade math teacher in a public school with a minimum of classroom experience under my belt.
My greatest challenge: how to maintain discipline while teaching pre-
algebra to students who had little interest in the subject.

Generally speaking, new teachers fall into one of two categories
when it comes to discipline. The Drill Sergeants start off the year using
overly strict measures in order to maintain stern and impersonal control over the students. On the opposite end of the spectrum, the
Popularity Contestants start off with a minimum of discipline, trying
to be liked by their students and hoping that respectful relationships
will result. Seasoned teachers, of course, have learned to find a wise and
practical balance between these two extremes.

Finding the right approach to discipline can be equally challenging
to us as positive moms. Depending on our personalities, we each tend
to implement slightly different philosophies in the training of our children. Even happily married spouses can differ as to the best form of
correction to use with their kids. But despite the variety of viewpoints

that exist, we can still identify several key principles for disciplining our children with love—I call it "affirmative training"—that can apply in every home.

Discipline should be a positive experience. Of course, it may not seem positive for the recipient at the time! But in the long run, if discipline is handled with love, it can effectively teach and train our kids to live effective, self-controlled, fulfilled lives. Now that's positive! Hebrews 12:11 says, "No discipline seems pleasant at the time, but painful. Later on, however, it produces a harvest of righteousness and peace for those who have been trained by it." Our goal in affirmative training is not to make discipline a *pleasant* experience for our children, but to teach and train them to live lives that honor God in a positive way.

Disciplining the Three *D*s

Wouldn't it be great to have a flow chart that could lead us through the issues of parenting and discipline? If our child does A, then we punish with B. If our child says this, then we respond with that. But there are no quick or easy methods. Godly discipline requires wisdom, discernment, and strong love in each new situation.

Fortunately the Bible has a great deal to say about our responsibility as parents to discipline our children, and God—our heavenly Father—provides us with a perfect example to follow. The Bible draws a clear comparison between God's discipline and the discipline we need to show to our own children:

> My son, do not make light of the Lord's discipline, and do not lose heart when he rebukes you, because the Lord disciplines those he loves, and he punishes everyone he accepts as a son.
>
> Endure hardships as discipline; God is treating you as sons. For what son is not disciplined by his father? If you are not disciplined

(and everyone undergoes discipline), then you are illegitimate children and not true sons.... Our fathers disciplined us for a little while as they thought best; but God disciplines us for our good, that we may share in his holiness. (Hebrews 12:5–10)

God, our wonderful heavenly Father, loves us—and therefore he disciplines us. He prods us and leads us for our own good. He disciplines us with a loving hand. I'm so thankful that God doesn't treat each one of us exactly the same, aren't you? He knows us individually. He understands the unique aspects of our sinful nature and lovingly disciplines us, using methods tailor-made for us.

We, too, can train our children with love, not anger or frustration. Affirmative training and discipline is based on the fact that we discipline those whom we love. Our children can rest in the assurance of our love when we show them that we care enough to take the time to lead them and correct them.

Getting to the Heart of the Matter

A large part of disciplining our children with love involves resisting the temptation to focus solely on correcting negative behavior. Instead, we must realize that our children's actions are an outgrowth of what is in their heart. Jesus said, "For from within, out of men's hearts, come evil thoughts, sexual immorality, theft, murder, adultery, greed, malice, deceit, lewdness, envy, slander, arrogance and folly" (Mark 7:21–22). He also said, "The good man brings good things out of the good stored up in his heart, and the evil man brings evil things out of the evil stored up in his heart. For out of the overflow of his heart his mouth speaks" (Luke 6:45).

Dealing with behavior only is like trying to put a bandage on the hurting arm of a man who is having a heart attack. The pain in the arm is a result of the heart problem, and a bandage won't fix the problem. As we lovingly discipline our children, we need to tend to their heart problem first.

In his book *Shepherding a Child's Heart,* Dr. Tedd Tripp encourages parents to learn to work back from a child's behavior to the heart issue—to expose the heart struggles involved in a certain behavior and help the child see that he or she has been created for a relationship with God.[1] Doing so requires effort, however, and a commitment to communicate with our children. Often, dealing with a behavior or a simple surface issue seems like the easier, quicker route. It's especially tempting when we're tired, angry, busy, or all three. But good communication— the kind that expends both time and effort to find out what is truly going on inside the hearts of our children—goes hand in hand with positive discipline.

Take the situation of an eleven-year-old daughter on a Sunday morning who is crying and begging not to go to church. The quick and easy response would be "Stop crying and get in the car. We are going to church whether you like it or not. Hurry up, because you are making us late."

But good communication that gets to the heart might sound more like this:

Mom: "Why are you crying?"

Daughter: "Because I'm having a bad hair day, and I don't want to go to church."

Mom: "I think your hair looks great. Does it really matter if your hair is not perfect?"

Daughter: "Yes! The seventh-grade girls in Sunday school make fun of us sixth graders. I don't want them to laugh at me because my hair is funny."

Mom: "So it's not that you don't want to go to church; you just don't want to face those girls with your less-than-perfect hair. Let's go on to church, because whether your hair looks perfect or not, we still need to go, right? Now let's talk about how you can have confidence with those seventh graders...."

Do you see how this mother is beginning to expose the heart issue here? She is following an important biblical principle: "Everyone should be quick to listen, slow to speak and slow to become angry, for man's anger does not bring about the righteous life that God desires" (James 1:19–20). Because she has made the extra effort to find out what is motivating her daughter's Sunday morning tantrum, this mom can now go on to encourage her daughter about feeling confident despite what others think or say. She can talk about the reason we go to church in the first place. She is still going to make her daughter go to church, but no doubt the girl will go with a much lighter heart than she would have under the first scenario. Both mother and daughter have learned something because they took the time to really communicate.

If our children are still toddlers, of course, we may not be able to get to the heart of a particular behavior through in-depth conversation. Still, we can take a moment to examine a situation and consider the possible underlying issues before rushing in and dealing only with the negative actions. Even at this early age, communication should go hand in hand with the discipline we apply. Younger children can be taught to understand the importance of choosing God's ways instead of their own way through loving, affirmative training.

Discipline for the Three *D*s

The word used for discipline in the Bible refers to the chastening, training, or instructing of our children. It is not to be confused with the

Parents must get across the idea that "I love you always, but sometimes I do not love your behavior." —Amy Vanderbilt

word for punishment. As we instruct and chasten our children, however, we may need to make use of punishment, particularly when it comes to three important areas of negative behavior. They are easily remembered as the three Ds: disobedience, disrespect, and dishonesty. Children must learn at an early age that negative consequences will follow any of the three Ds.

The Bible confirms the effectiveness of punishment in such cases. Proverbs 22:15 says, "Folly is bound up in the heart of a child, but the rod of discipline will drive it far from him." Some people, citing this verse, believe in using an actual rod (or wooden spoon or paddle) to administer punishment, while others believe the "rod of discipline" refers to punishment in general. Either way, one thing is clear: punishment needs to hurt in order to be effective in stopping negative behavior. Remember the passage from Hebrews 12 that we cited earlier? Discipline is not pleasant; it's painful. But the end result is "righteousness and peace for those who have been trained by it" (v. 11).

Six-year-old Susan had an attitude of disrespect for her mother, disobeying and talking back to her on a regular basis. Susan's mom tried to stay on top of the situation, using what she thought was loving discipline with each infraction. If Susan spoke disrespectfully, her mom would respond, "Off to your room for another ten minute time-out!" But over time Susan's behavior did not improve; in fact, it got worse. Why? Because Susan loved to go to her room and play with her dolls and toys. Not only did her punishment not hurt, she enjoyed it!

We must carefully consider the form of punishment we use with our children. If a particular penalty doesn't seem to bother the recipient, we need to come up with something else. We need to ask, "What motivates this child—and what will hurt enough to provoke a positive change?"

Even children within the same family may require different forms of punishment. In my home, one of my daughters is money-motivated. I have learned that an effective punishment for her is to take away some of her allowance. She will feel it painfully! My other daughter, however, could care less if I took away her allowance. For her, real pain is to miss out on one of her favorite television shows. Knowing their differences in interest and motivation helps me administer punishment that works.

Whatever form of punishment you choose, however, you can enhance its effectiveness by following three steps.

1. Communicate with your children. Make sure they understand why they are being punished. Have them repeat to you, "I am being punished because _____." This not only helps them understand the purpose of the punishment, it also allows them an opportunity to confess their guilt. Make an effort to examine the heart issue behind the negative behavior and search out some scriptures that can be applied to the situation.

2. Punish immediately and without anger. The punishment for the behavior should be meted out as soon after the offense as possible. Set a limit—say, "ten minutes in time-out" or "no telephone for the weekend." Then follow through and be consistent. Ephesians 6:4 reminds us, "Do not exasperate you children; instead, bring them up in the training and instruction of the Lord." Many parents make the mistake of handing down a lengthy or open-ended punishment that they will either forget about or not be able to follow through on. A long, drawn-out punishment loses its effectiveness. Make the penalty short, immediate, and effective.

3. Renew the relationship. Once the punishment has been administered, it is important to make sure your children know they are loved and forgiven. This does not detract from the punishment, but rather reminds them that although you love them, you don't approve of their behavior. They need to know your love is not performance-based, just as God's love is not performance-based. Pray together, asking God to help them to overcome the temptation to repeat the wrong behavior.

Positive Motivation

According to some schools of thought, parents should never use negative discipline; we should use only positive reinforcement to train our children. But as we have already seen, that is not God's philosophy. In addition to the Scripture passages we've already mentioned, the Book of Proverbs talks often about using "the rod of discipline" (for example, in Proverbs 10:13; 22:15; and 23:13–14).

Still, there are times when positive reinforcement can be used to motivate children in a certain direction. We might, for example, offer them a reward for good grades or for keeping their room straight all week. If we overuse positive reinforcement, however, our kids can become programmed to expect a prize for everything they do. This approach encourages selfish tendencies and a mentality that says, "I will only do it if there is something in it for me." We need to teach our children from an early age that many acts of service in life should be done just because we ought to be givers, not takers.

I know. You don't want to be known as a "mean" mom. Me either. Our kids will not always agree with the discipline we use; but trust me, they will come to appreciate it in time! As evidence, read the following essay, published October 28, 1999, on CNSNews.com. The author is unknown:

> We had the meanest mother in the whole world!
>
> While other kids ate candy for breakfast, we had to have cereal, eggs, and toast. When others had a Pepsi and a Twinkie for lunch,

we had to eat sandwiches. And you can guess our mother fixed us a dinner that was different from what other kids had too.

Mother insisted on knowing where we were at all times. You'd think we were convicts in a prison. She had to know who our friends were and what we were doing with them. She insisted that if we said we would be gone for an hour, we would be gone for an hour or less.

We were ashamed to admit it, but she had the nerve to break the Child Labor Laws by making us work. WE had to wash the dishes, make the beds, learn to cook, vacuum the floor, do laundry, and all sorts of cruel jobs. I think she would lie awake at night thinking of more things for us to do.

She always insisted on us telling the truth, the whole truth, and nothing but the truth. By the time we were teenagers, she could read our minds.

Then, life was really tough! Mother wouldn't let our friends just honk the horn when they drove up. They had to come up to the door so she could meet them. While everyone else could date when they were 12 or 13, we had to wait until we were 16.

Because of our mother we missed out on lots of things other kids experienced. None of us have ever been caught shoplifting, vandalizing other's property, or ever arrested for any crime. It was all her fault.

Now that we have left home, we are all God-fearing, educated, honest adults. We are doing our best to be mean parents just like mom was. I think that's what's wrong with the world today. It just doesn't have enough mean moms anymore.

What about you? Are you a mean mom? If we're going by the definition above, I hope so! A positive mom lovingly disciplines her children.

She examines the heart issues and trains her kids to live obedient lives that glorify God. She uses punishment with wisdom and discernment. She uses positive reinforcement carefully. The results are not guaranteed, but the potential for blessing and fulfillment is enormous. As Proverbs 6:23 says, "For these commands are a lamp, this teaching is a light, and the corrections of discipline are the way to life."

POWER POINT

Read: Genesis 3, the story of Adam and Eve as they disobeyed God. Notice how God handled the situation through communication, punishment, and forgiveness.

Pray: How wonderful you are, Almighty God! You are the perfect Father. Help me to learn to discipline through your example. Help me to be wise and discerning as I train my children, and may their hearts be drawn to you in the process. Give me the courage and the love to discipline, even when it's not popular to do so. May my children grow to honor you with their lives. In Jesus' name, amen.

Do: Set aside a time with each child in which you talk about God's love and his guidelines for living. Help them to understand that when they disobey or show disrespect or dishonesty, they are stepping out of God's plan, and consequences will follow. Read Psalm 25 together.

Conclusion

Upward Bound
Continuing to Grow in the Schoolroom of Life

For the LORD gives wisdom, and from his mouth come knowledge and
understanding. He holds victory in store for the upright, he is a shield
to those whose walk is blameless, for he guards the course of the just
and protects the way of his faithful ones.
—Proverbs 2:6–8

"No fair. *You* don't have to go to school." I hear these words from my kids quite often these days. I remember saying them to *my* mom, too, especially during those challenging junior high years when it seemed as though school would never end. But the truth is, I am still in a classroom. You are too. It may not look like the classrooms we remember, with desks, chairs, and blackboards. But life is its own kind of classroom, and we are in the continuing education course called Motherhood 101.

Each day we take in new knowledge, building on the lessons we've learned from both our mistakes and our victories. Experience is one of our teachers, but there are others. Our friends, family members, and mentor moms are excellent teaching assistants, and we learn from their wisdom and example. Books on parenting—ranging in topic matter from effective discipline to potty training—also help. Then there are the two important instructors God provides: his Word and his Holy Spirit. These represent two sources of powerful wisdom for our daily lives.

Do the classes ever stop? No. The curriculum may change, but we will never arrive at the point where we can say, "Now I know it all." We may move on to courses such as Empty Nest 101 and Grandmotherhood 101, but we are still assimilating new information and experiences. When we're faced with new challenges, we need to tell ourselves the same thing we tell our kids when they face difficult times in their studies: "Don't give up! Don't be discouraged when you make a mistake! Grow from it, learn from it, and become better because of it!"

In the introduction you read a Bible verse that is my theme scripture as a positive mom: "A wise woman builds her house" (Proverbs 14:1). As this verse indicates, you and I are builders. We are shapers of our children's world. We set the attitude and atmosphere in our homes. Yes, we make mistakes along the way, but we can use our failures as opportunities to learn and grow and become better, more positive moms.

How does a positive woman build her home? One brick at a time! She uses bricks of support and encouragement, of positive discipline, of loving forgiveness. She uses bricks formed from her positive example in word and deed. To these, she adds bricks of strong moral conviction based on the foundation of God's Word. She never forgets the important bricks of daily prayer. And, of course, she sets the Lord Jesus Christ as the cornerstone for the whole building.

The wise woman who builds her house is not the only woman mentioned in Proverbs 14:1, however. Solomon, the writer of Proverbs, also describes the foolish woman: "With her own hands the foolish one tears [her house] down." How does a foolish woman tear down her home? Whining and complaining are two destructive influences that come to mind off the bat. Anger and bitterness are another two that have the potential to destroy a marriage and a home. Then there are the negative influences that a foolish woman allows to enter her home through the media or through friends, chipping away at the foundation of God's moral standards. A foolish woman does not use discernment in limiting her children's exposure to these destructive influences.

A foolish mother's example is reckless and harmful, leading to faithlessness and moral decay among her family members. She is too busy to pray. In fact, she is too busy for many things. A foolish woman tends to overload her schedule with activities and interests that make her tired, frazzled, and irritable. She continually screams her demands at her children instead of gently prodding them and training them in the way they should go.

A foolish woman has forgotten her power source. She relies on her own strength instead of leaning on God's abiding love and help.

No Regrets

We all have regrets as mothers. We know what we could have done differently or what could have been said with a more even temper. But recognizing that we all make mistakes, we must forgive ourselves and move on. God has forgiven us through Christ; how can we do less? "Regret is an appalling waste of energy; you can't build on it; it's only good for wallowing in," says Katherine Mansfield.[1] Instead of wallowing in regret, we must learn from our mistakes, commit to doing better, and keep moving forward.

Of course, we don't use the fact that we are forgiven as an excuse to continue in mistakes or wrongdoing. True repentance means that we turn from our sin 180 degrees and go in the other direction. But once we turn in that opposite direction, we start walking. The apostle Paul was a man who had many reasons for regret. Before he became a believer, he persecuted Christians and even helped put some to death. Paul could have spent the rest of his life wallowing in sorrow for what he had done, crushed under the overwhelming weight of guilt and remorse. Most likely, he did grieve over what he had done—but then he moved on. He was confident that God had a plan for his life, and he made himself available for that purpose.

In Philippians 3:12–14 we find Paul's famous statement about moving forward and not looking back. He declared that he wasn't perfect—just faithful in following God's direction for his life. Can you relate Paul's message to your personal calling as a mother?

> Not that I have already obtained all this, or have already been made perfect, but I press on to take hold of that for which Christ Jesus took hold of me. Brothers, I do not consider myself yet to have taken hold of it. But one thing I do: Forgetting what is behind and straining toward what is ahead, I press on toward the goal to win the prize for which God has called me heavenward in Christ Jesus.

God has given us a high calling as mothers that can be summed up this way: *Our calling is to honor Christ in raising our families and building our homes.* This brief sentence encompasses the many roles we have in life—wife, mother, nurturer, teacher, disciplinarian, and so much more. Notice our job is to honor Christ, not to create perfect kids. The results of our efforts are not up to us, they are up to God. As we stay connected to him as our power source and employ the principles he sets forth in his Word, the Bible, we will become the positive moms we want to be.

As we come to the end of this book, my prayer is that the seven principles I've shared with you will give you the encouragement and direction you need to continue on your journey of positive motherhood. Think of this book as a midday snack—an energy bar or power shake. It's not your main course or primary source of nutrition. Rather, it's a supplement—a healthy one, I hope—to your daily intake of God's nourishing Word.

Perhaps you are in the early years of parenting and need a positive "shot in the arm" to help you through these beginning stages. Perhaps you are midway through the mothering years, or even approaching the end, and you need an extra boost of encouragement to make it to the finish line. Whatever your circumstances, you can continue onward and upward by applying these seven power-packed principles of a positive mom:

1. Seize every opportunity to give encouragement.

2. Stay in prayer.

3. Stop whining and keep a positive attitude.

4. Strengthen your relationships with family, friends, and mentors.

5. Set a good example.

6. Seek God's standards in life.

7. Send a message of love and forgiveness.

May the Lord bless you and give you wisdom and strength as you build your house. And may your children, your family members, your friends, and all those around you see in your life the power of a positive mom!

POWER POINT

⚙ **Read:** Philippians 2–4. What positive encouragement does Paul give you? What warnings does he mention? How does this scripture passage help you to be a better mother?

♡ **Pray:** Wonderful heavenly Father, you are the king of heaven, the Alpha and Omega, the creator of the universe. How wonderful to know that you are willing to help me in my home! Help me to be a positive mother. Forgive me for my past mistakes and sins. Thank you for your forgiveness through Jesus. Help me to press on in a positive direction, blessing and building my home and family. Thank you for being my power source and never leaving me. Thank you for helping me in this incredible journey of motherhood. In Jesus' name I pray. Amen.

☺ **Do:** Skim back through the pages of this book, highlighting the points you especially need to remember. Ask God to specifically help you in applying these principles to your life. Commit to reading the most important instruction book (the Bible) every day.

Notes

Chapter 1: Influence beyond Measure

1. Susan Lapinski, *God Can Handle It for Mothers* (Nashville, Tenn.: Brighton Books, 1998), 23.

2. Information courtesy of Ric Edelman, author of the national bestsellers *The Truth about Money* and *The New Rules of Money*. Edelman also hosts a weekly radio show and a live call-in television show in the Washington, D.C., area. His firm, Edelman Financial Services, Inc., is located in Fairfax, Virginia. For additional information, see his Web site at www.ricedelman.com.

3. Thomas Huang and Karen M. Thomas, "Do Parents Rule?" *Dallas Morning News,* 7 September 1998, 1C.

4. As reprinted in *God's Little Devotional Book for Moms* (Tulsa, Okla.: Honor Books, 1995), 113. First published in *The Bible Friend*. The poem's author is unknown.

5. Mabel Bartlett and Sophia Baker, *Mothers—Makers of Men* (New York: Exposition Press, 1952), 92.

Chapter 2: The Secret to Your Success

1. Edyth Draper, *Draper's Book of Quotations for the Christian World* (Wheaton, Ill.: Tyndale House, 1992), entry #3884.

2. *The Laurel Instant Quotation Dictionary* (Mundelein, Ill.: Career Publishing, 1972), 246.

3. Carlene Ward, *God Can Handle It for Mother* (Nashville, Tenn.: Brighton Books, 1998), 114.

Chapter 3: Apples of Gold

1. Abigail Van Buren, "Dear Abby," *Dallas Morning News* (10 January 1999), 6F.

2. Glen Van Ekeren, *Speakers Sourcebook II* (Englewood Cliffs, N. J.: Prentice Hall, 1994), 124.

3. Ibid., 123.

4. Evelyn L. Beilenson, comp., *First Aid for a Mother's Soul* (White Plains, N. Y.: Peter Pauper Press, Inc.1998), 52.

Chapter 4: Great Expectations

1. Summer Sanders, *Champions Are Raised, Not Born* (New York: Random House, Inc., 1999), 5.

2. *Bless Your Heart, Series II* (Eden Prairie, Minn.: Heartland Samplers, Inc., 1990), 3.2.

3. Sanders, *Champions Are Raised, Not Born*, 22.

4. Van Ekeren, *Speakers Sourcebook II*, 174.

5. Donald Clifton, "A Predictive Validity Study of the Basketball Player In-Depth Interview" (The Gallop Organization, 1988).

Chapter 5: The Beauty of a Smile

1. Dale Carnegie, *How to Win Friends & Influence People* (New York: Pocket Books, 1981), 69–70.

2. Michael Collopy, *Works of Love Are Works of Peace* (Fort Collins, Colo.: Ignatius Press, 1996), 123, 125.

Chapter 6: A Positive Mom Is a Praying Mom

1. *God's Little Devotional Book for Moms*, 77.

2. Collopy, *Works of Love Are Works of Peace*, 103.

3. John Blanchard, comp., *More Gathered Gold* (Hertfordshire, England: Evangelical Press, 1986), 233.

4. Ibid., 234.

Chapter 7: Casting Your Cares

1. Van Ekeren, *The Speaker's Sourcebook II*, 399.

2. Ibid.

3. Corrie ten Boom with John and Elizabeth Sherrill, *The Hiding Place* (New York: Bantam Books, 1974), 29.

4. O. Hallesby, translated by Clarence J. Carlsen, "What Is Prayer?" *Intercessor*, Coral Ridge Ministries (November 1990, Volume 1, Number 3), 1.

Chapter 8: Women of Prayer

1. Lindsey O'Connor, *Moms Who Changed the World* (Eugene, Ore.: Harvest House Publishers, 1999), 49–61.

2. *God's Little Devotional Book for Moms*, 231.

3. Blanchard, *More Gathered Gold*, 232.

4. Ralph S. Cushman, *Spiritual Hilltops: A Pocket Prayer Book* (Nashville, Tenn.: Upper Room Press, 1941), 49.

5. Blanchard, *More Gathered Gold*, 232.

Chapter 9: The Ladies Pity Party

1. Van Ekeren, *Speakers Sourcebook II,* 47.

Chapter 10: Attitude of Gratitude

1. Charles R. Swindoll, *Strengthening Your Grip* (Nashville, Tenn.: Word Inc., 1982), 206.
2. Used with permission of the author.
3. Eleanor H. Porter, *Pollyanna* (Boston, Mass.: Colonial Press, 1920), 43–45.
4. Colleen O'Connor, "Smile, Smile, Smile," *Dallas Morning News,* 25 March 2000, 1G.

Chapter 11: The Challenges of Life

1. Van Ekeren, *Speakers Sourcebook,* 26.
2. Kenneth W. Osbeck, *101 Hymn Stories* (Grand Rapids, Mich.: Kregel Publications, 1982), 145.
3. Ibid., 26.
4. Jack Canfield, Mark Victor Hansen, Jennifer Read Hawthorne, Marci Shimoff, *Chicken Soup for the Mother's Soul* (Deerfield Beach, Fla.: Health Communications, Inc., 1997), 113–14.

Chapter 12: Harmony with Hubby

1. Gary D. Chapman, *The Five Languages of Love: How to Express Heartfelt Commitment to Your Mate* (Northfield Publishers, 1996).
2. James C. Dobson, *Love Must Be Tough: Proven Hope for Families in Crisis* (Nashville, Tenn.: Word, 1996).

Chapter 13: Affirming Friendships

1. Alan Loy McGinnis, *The Friendship Factor* (Minneapolis, Minn.: Augsburg Publishing House, 1979), 25.
2. *The Laurel Instant Quotation Dictionary,* 139.

Chapter 15: Living Lesson Books

1. *The Never Ending Story* (Warner Brothers Family Entertainment, 1984).
2. Van Ekeren, *Speakers Sourcebook II,* 135.
3. Bil Keane, "The Family Circus," *Dallas Morning News,* Sunday, 16 January 2000.
4. Croft M. Pentz, ed., *The Speakers Treasury of 400 Quotable Poems* (Grand Rapids, Mich.: Zondervan Publishing House, 1963), 159.

Chapter 17: Living by the Book

1. From correspondence with author.
2. Josh McDowell, *Right from Wrong* (Dallas, Tex.: Word Publishing, 1994), 12.
3. *God's Little Devotional Book for Moms,* 39.
4. William J. Johnstone, *George Washington the Christian* (Milford, Mich.: Mott Media, 1985), 19.
5. Ibid.
6. W. Herbert Burk, F.D., *Washington's Prayers* (Norristown, Penn.: Published for the Benefit of the Washington Memorial Chapel, 1907), 87–95.

Chapter 18: Legacies in Literature

1. *God's Little Devotional Book for Moms,* 38.
2. William J. Bennett, Chester Finn, and John Cribb, *The Educated Child* (New York: The Free Press, 1999), 534.
3. Linda Karges-Bone, Ed.D., "A New Look at Old Books," *Christian Parenting Today,* July/August 1996, 24.
4. Ibid., 192.
5. Ibid., 193.

Chapter 20: Affirmative Training

1. Dr. Ted Tripp, *Shepherding a Child's Heart* (Wapwallopen, Penn.: Shepherd Press, 1995).

Conclusion: Upward Bound

1. *The Laurel Instant Quotation Dictionary,* 253.